The Electra airliner was a pilot's dream, the mistress, sweetheart, or wife of virutally every man who flew it. The Electra was better than any other plane in history. It had enormous reserve power, handled smoothly and responsively, was fast and versatile, and was forgiving of mistakes. It was a pilot's airplane.

And then one warm, humid night, a Texas farmer and his wife were jolted out of bed by a massive metallic, snarling, tortured noise. They raced outside to see an airliner that had, without warning, disintegrated in mid-air.

A few months later, in broad daylight and clear weather, another Electra arrowed into an Indiana soybean field. A cauldron of mangled wreckage and human bodies seethed and burned for five days.

And in the hue and cry it seemed inevitable that the Electras would have to be grounded.

But the head of the Federal Aviation Agency—Elwood R. Quesada, a former Air Force general and hot-shot fighter pilot—only ordered speed restrictions for the Electras.

Which was an incredible gamble. Because if Quesada did not solve the greatest aviation mystery of all time, and another Electra went down, all of commercial aviation— and particularly one Elwood R. Quesada—would be irreparably damaged.

D1555091

# THE BANTAM AIR & SPACE SERIES

To Fly Like the Eagles . . .

It took some 1800 years for mankind to win mastery of a challenging and life-threatening environment—the sea. In just under 70 years we have won mastery of an even more hostile environment—the air. In doing so, we have realized a dream as old as man—to be able to fly.

The Bantam Air & Space series consists of books that focus on the skills of piloting—from the days when the Wright brothers made history at Kitty Hawk to the era of barnstorming daredevils of the sky, through the explosion of technology, design, and flyers that occurred in World War II, and finally to the cool daring of men who first broke the sound barrier, walked the Moon, and have lived and worked in space stations—always at high risk, always proving the continued need for their presence and skill.

The Air & Space series will be published once a month as mass market books with special illustrations, and with varying lengths and prices. Aviation enthusiasts would be wise to buy each book as it comes out if they are to collect the complete Library.

# THE
# ELECTRA STORY
## AVIATION'S GREATEST MYSTERY

Robert J. Serling

**BANTAM BOOKS**

NEW YORK · TORONTO · LONDON · SYDNEY · AUCKLAND

THE ELECTRA STORY: AVIATION'S GREATEST MYSTERY

*A Bantam Falcon Book / published by arrangement with
the author*

**PRINTING HISTORY**
*Originally published by Doubleday in 1963
Bantam edition / February 1991*

FALCON *and the portrayal of a boxed "f" are trademarks of Bantam Books,
a division of Bantam Doubleday Dell Publishing Group, Inc.*

Bantam Books are published by Bantam Books, a division of Bantam Doubleday
Dell Publishing Group, Inc. Its trademark, consisting of the words "Bantam
Books" and the portrayal of a rooster, is Registered in U.S. Patent and Trademark
Office and in other countries. Marca Registrada. Bantam Books, 666 Fifth Avenue,
New York, New York 10103.

## DEDICATION

To the memory of the crew, Braniff International Airways Flight 542, September 29, 1959:

Captain Wilson Stone
First Officer Dan Hollowell
Second Officer Roland Longhill
Stewardess Avilyn Harrison
Stewardess Betty Rusch
Stewardess Leona Winkler

And the crew of Northwest Orient Airlines Flight 710, March 17, 1960:

Captain Edgar LaParle
First Officer Joseph Mills
Flight Engineer Arnold Kowal
Stewardess Constance Nutter
Stewardess Barbara Schreiber
Flight Attendant Mitchell Foster

In life, they shared a common love of the air and pride in its daily conquest.

In death, they shared the ultimate truth of aviation—that from tragedy stems the inevitable reform and progress which must be part of that conquest.

# Contents

*Lockheed Electra (1959)*

# Author's Preface

This is the story of an airliner. The most praised and
pilloried, the most damned and defended commercial transport in the history of commercial aviation.

One pilot I talked to called it "absolutely the greatest
plane I ever flew and the safest in the air today, including
even the jets."

Another pilot told me, "I wouldn't fly the damned thing
from Idlewild to Newark."

Which may give you a general idea of what you are
about to read.

One person wrote this book; many helped, including
those who quite naturally would have preferred that it not
be written. I refer specifically to public relations officials
and engineers of the Lockheed Aircraft Corporation and
the Allison Division of General Motors. It is to their
everlasting credit that in no way whatsoever did they
attempt to censor the product, refuse cooperation, or duck
a single question. They have not only my utmost gratitude
but also my heartfelt admiration.

The author's chief acknowledgments, therefore, go to
J.F. McBrearty, Ben Cook, Preble Staver, Jack Real, Her-
man "Fish" Salmon, Ellis Stafford, Hall Hibbard, Grover
Nobles, and Erik Miller of Lockheed; Roger Fleming,
Fred Steuber, Bob Hicks, and John Whitmore of Allison.

A special word of thanks is due Elwood R. Quesada, former administrator of the Federal Aviation Agency, without whose cooperation some facets of the story could not have been told. The same accolade goes to Donald Nyrop, president of Northwest Orient Airlines; Edward Slattery, of the Civil Aeronautics Board's Bureau of Safety; Oscar Bakke, now Eastern Regional Administrator of the Federal Aviation Agency; and Brad Dunbar, formerly of *Aviation Daily*—a newspaperman I am proud to call a friend as well as a colleague.

To the following members of the following organizations, I can only express the hope that the book is worth the help they gave its author:

From American Airlines—Frank Brunton, Captain Art Weidman, Willis Player, William Littlewood, Stewardess Ginger Kent, and Ted MacEachen.

From the Air Line Pilots Association—Chet Spurgeon, Ted Linnert, Carl Eck, Tom Basnight, and Donna Lee Krusz.

From the Federal Aviation Agency—Administrator Najeeb E. Halaby, Joseph Hornsby, Phil Swatek, Howard Bingham, Craig Lewis, and Chris Nyhaug.

From Eastern Air Lines—Captain Edward Bechtold, Captain "Slim" Cockes, and Captain James Furr.

From Northwest Airlines—Captain Warren Avenson, Captain Jim Borden, Captain Robert Rockwell, Captain Don Schulberg, Stewardess Valerie Thorpe, and Director of Public Relations Bill Pollock.

From Braniff—Captain Homer Mouden and Captain Len Morgan.

From Pacific Southwest Airlines—Seymour Francis.

From *Flying* magazine—Bob Stanfield and Lou Davis.

From NASA—John Stack and Joe Stein.

From Aero Commander—Jerrie Cobb.

From the Air Transport Association—Dan Priest and Tom McGarry.

From United Press International—Preston McGraw, Stan Hall, and Hank Reiger.

From non-Electra airlines—Captain Robert Buck, Trans World; Captain John McDonald, United; and Captain Howard Kelly, Piedmont.

From Revell, Inc., Henry Blankfort.

To the paragon of efficiency who typed the manuscript, Patricia Gray, my fervent gratitude.

There are two other persons who aided immensely in the preparation of this book. One is my editor at Doubleday, Ellin K. Roberts, whose friendship I treasure and whose advice I should take more often. The other is my brother Rod.

Washington, D.C.
June, 1962

# Prologue

It all began on a warm, humid night—September 29, 1959.

A farmer named Richard E. White, too sleepy to watch the eleven o'clock news on television, turned off the set and yawned his way to the bedroom. His wife was already asleep.

Their forty-nine-acre farm was only a few miles from the tiny town of Buffalo, Texas (population 1200). Their children, grown up, lived and worked in Dallas. The Whites themselves had moved from Dallas to find more quiet. Their lives were peaceful, content, and prosaic—until the precise moment of 11:08 P.M., when White, his eyes heavy with drowsiness, jolted to attention.

He didn't see the garish, blinding, weird yellow light that filled the sky outside. But he heard the sound. Metallic, snarling, tortured, vibrating in his eardrums.

The startled White jumped out of bed and ran outside without bothering with his shoes. The entire sky seemed on fire, then suddenly faded as if a monstrous Roman candle had spent itself. White's wife had just run out to join him when a clap like thunder shook the earth. White put his arm around her in a gesture of futile protection and stared into the night, wondering and waiting.

Out of the black sky came a new sound—shrill, deafening whistles pitched to different keys. Next a roar—faint at first, then mushrooming into the approach of a thousand freight trains. Like two helpless, frightened children, the Whites huddled close together.

Heavy metal objects began crashing about them. The clamor ceased and the night was still again.

"It's raining," said Mrs. White incredulously.

"It couldn't be," her husband muttered. "Look at the stars."

But it apparently *was* raining. Gently, but most perceptibly. White sniffed the air suspiciously.

"That's not rain," he said. "It's—it's like coal oil."

In his bare feet he ran toward his vegetable patch, where most of the objects had fallen. It was littered with pieces of torn aluminum and strips of yellow insulating material. White turned his horrified eyes toward a tree close to his pigpen a few yards away.

There, resting in the branches, white and gleaming, was the huge rudder of an aircraft. On it were some red letters. It suddenly dawned on farmer White what had fallen from the skies.

"FLY BRANIFF," the letters said.

The "rain" White thought smelled like coal oil was kerosene. Fuel for jet-powered engines. And the rudder in the tree by his pigpen belonged to Braniff International Airways Flight 542, an L-188.

Otherwise known as the Lockheed Electra.

# 1

# The Electra Is Born

Go back three decades—to another warm fall night in the year 1932, to an aircraft plant in Burbank, California.

A young Lockheed aeronautical engineer named Hall L. Hibbard looked up from his blueprints and was surprised to find his attractive wife, Irene, standing there.

"Hi," she said. "I knew you'd be working late again so I thought I'd come down and keep you company."

Hibbard smiled and went back to his blueprints. Irene Hibbard watched for a while, sipped some coffee, curled up on a big unused drawing board, and went to sleep.

Just behind her, sleek and shining under the bright lights, an airplane was taking shape. Soon it would travel the skies as one of the world's first all-metal, twin-engine, low-wing transport planes. It bore the technical name of Lockheed Model 10. But, like virtually every plane Lockheed had built since the mid-twenties and early thirties, it also carried the name of a star. There had been the Orion, Vega, Sirius, Altair.

This one would be called the Electra. And on her rested the entire hopes of the fledgling company, reorganized only a few months after its parent company, Detroit Aircraft, had sunk into bankruptcy.

Lockheed itself had been organized only six years before, by pilot-aeronautical engineer Allan Lockheed. Despite the fast-growing reputation of his planes, he ran into

*Lockheed Electra (1932)*

tough financial sledding. In 1929 he merged Lockheed with Detroit Aircraft, actually a holding company, and stepped out.

The little Burbank factory tried valiantly to operate under the twin handicaps of absentee ownership and the worldwide depression. But Detroit Aircraft itself folded, and the Lockheed Aircraft Corporation followed it into bankruptcy.

On June 6, 1932, thirty-five-year-old Robert Ellsworth Gross walked into the U.S. District Court in Los Angeles and offered $40,000 for the assets of the bankrupt Burbank company. Gross, who had worked for other aircraft firms but wanted one of his own, raised the money with six other adventuresome men, including a Lockheed executive named Carl Squier.

Squier had been running Lockheed until it went broke through no fault of his own. The preceding Christmas Eve, as the disheartened employees filed out of the plant,

Squier had been at the gate to wish them a Merry Christmas—and hand each of the one hundred and twenty workers a ten-dollar bill. The money was the last of his own personal savings.

The following January he had to mortgage his car and home to meet the payroll. When Lockheed went into bankruptcy a few months later, Squier's final payroll consisted of three persons—a secretary, an accountant, and a stockroom clerk who also doubled as night watchman.

At the moment Gross walked into the courtroom to enter his $40,000 bid, the name Lockheed already was a proud one in America's infant aircraft industry. Its traditional "Winged Star" emblazoned ships that from 1928 through 1931 broke virtually every speed and distance record on the books. The names of pilots flying Lockheed equipment were household words. Frank Hawks. Ruth Nichols. Roscoe Turner. Charles Lindbergh. And a former Lockheed test pilot named Wiley Post who flew a Vega

*Winnie Mae*

christened *Winnie Mae* around the world in only eight days.

In effect, Gross and his six associates were purchasing a reputation and nothing else. The bankruptcy inventory added up to less than $130,000, most of it consisting of a few spare parts, machine tools, furniture, and a pencil sharpener listed at fifty cents. There also was a one-hundred-and-seventy-one-dollar safe, with nothing inside it.

There were no competing bids, although Gross had an anxious moment when he spotted Allan Lockheed in the courtroom. The founder, however, had been unable to raise enough funds to buy back his company and the judge approved the sale with the wry comment:

"I hope you know what you're doing."

It was Gross who hired Hibbard, regarded as one of the best designers in the business even though the young engineer never learned to fly himself. Hibbard's first assignment was to create a single-engine, all-metal passenger plane carrying ten persons. But Gross got another idea.

He was eating breakfast one morning at the old Union Air Terminal in Burbank when he spotted three planes parked outside. One was a Lockheed Orion, the second a Ford trimotor, and the third Boeing's new twin-engine transport, the 247. Gross thought to himself, "Which plane would I choose if I were going to fly to San Francisco?" He gulped down his coffee, drove over to the two-story former ranch house that was Lockheed's executive building, and stuck his head into Hibbard's office.

"Let's junk what we're doing and put two engines on it," he told his chief designer.

When it came time to name the new project, Gross went to the Burbank public library and pored through astronomy books. He wanted to retain Lockheed's system for naming its planes after stars. He finally settled on Electra, the so-called "lost" star of the Pleiades, named after the mythological Greek goddess who became a comet and wandered eternally through the heavens.

Development costs on the new transport mounted alarmingly. At one point the new firm's credit standing was so shaky that packages addressed to Lockheed were delivered C.O.D.

No romantic thoughts about past history were in Hall Hibbard's mind as he struggled over the blueprints. Of more import was the fact that the Electra was Lockheed's first venture into the multiengine transport field and its most important single project. If the Model 10 flopped, so would Lockheed.

Hibbard looked at his sleeping wife for a moment and shook his head in a gesture of pride mingled with guilt. Then he resumed his work.

"I still think we may have trouble with that rudder setup," he said to a colleague. "Now suppose we . . ."

It took Hibbard and eleven other men a year to design the first Electra. Only one year elapsed between the original blueprint and the initial test flight. Twenty-five years later, the Electra of the jet age was the product of nearly one thousand engineers and two years of work between blueprint and test-flight stages.

In 1932 Hibbard required only one drawing to detail the entire electrical system of the old Electra. The plane that flew twenty-five years later needed one thousand separate drawings for its electrical innards. For the first Electra, one man did all the stress analysis—determining what key structural parts will do under various strains and loads of flight. A typical structural test involved somebody pushing a foot against a piece of tubing to see if it would hold. The Electra of a quarter century later had more than 300 engineers and equipment costing millions of dollars assigned to this one phase of testing.

When the 1932 Electra made her first flight, Hibbard waited anxiously on the ground for the verdict of a single person—test pilot Marshall Headle. Headle landed and broke Hibbard's heart.

*Ford Tri-Motor*

"She's nice, but the rudder forces are lousy," he reported bluntly.

Hibbard went back to work redesigning the Electra's twin rudders. Thirty years later, he recalled the incident as another reminder of how aviation has progressed.

"We used to depend solely on the word of the test pilot," he said. "He told us 'she flies good' or 'she flies bad.' His reaction was all we had to go on. Now the pilot is just one cog in the test program. Every time he moves his hands or feet in a new airplane, the results are recorded on machines and graphs. We're interested in a pilot's reactions, of course, but we wouldn't dare evaluate a plane's performance on what one man feels through the seat of his pants."

Despite that relatively primitive method of determining whether "she flies good or bad," however, the Model 10 was an almost immediate success. The first Electra carried a price tag of $50,000, which wouldn't pay for one of her successor's Allison engines. United States airlines ordered nearly 150, and the Electra was the first American-built transport to find a large market among foreign carriers.

Before the orders began rolling in, the Electra gave its then-youthful designer a few final moments of concern. Headle had just finished putting the plane through its final Civil Aeronautics Authority certification tests and radioed Hibbard he was coming in.

"We'll have a celebration tonight," Headle announced gleefully as he banked the trim transport over the Burbank airport and swung into his approach.

But as the ship came in, Hibbard's heart went into his mouth. One wheel still was retracted, and in 1932 engineers had yet to come up with a device to lower a stuck gear manually. Hibbard knew a crash was inevitable and that there was nothing anyone could do. It also happened to be the only Electra built and the plane Lockheed was going to use for sales demonstrations. In about thirty seconds there wasn't going to be any Electra.

Headle did a beautiful job of landing on one wheel, but eventually a wing had to touch ground and that was it. Luckily damage was not too severe, the plane was repaired, and Carl Squier, now a key sales executive in the reorganized company, started selling the nation's newest transport aircraft.

One thing should be remembered about the early sales efforts and the original Electra itself. In those days Lockheed and other manufacturers literally told the airlines what they wanted and needed. Twenty-five years later they had found they could not sell an airliner merely by building it first and then hoping someone would like it well enough to buy it.

Lockheed's second Electra project dates back to 1953 when Capital Airlines approached the Burbank firm on the possibility of designing a turboprop (jet engines hitched to conventional propellers) airliner. Capital, however, primarily was interested in a short-haul plane and Lockheed's engineers were not too enthusiastic about the prospects. They were thinking of a bigger, more versatile aircraft, and in 1954 American Airlines laid down the specifications for a new type of commercial transport along those lines. Eastern also expressed interest, although at first glance what they wanted literally was an aeronautical moon.

Give us, said American's hard-bitten president C.R. Smith, a turboprop ship that can:

—Cruise easily at speeds of more than 400 miles per hour,

—Operate profitably on flights as short as 100 miles and as long as 2700 miles,

—Carry at least sixty-five passengers,

—Take off fast enough and land slowly enough to serve any of the nation's 100 major airports, large and small—particularly fields that never would be able to handle the forthcoming pure jets.

What American and Eastern were seeking was the most versatile airliner ever designed. There was nothing like it flying or, for that matter, on any drawing board. American said literally:

"This is what we want. Can anyone build it?"

Britain proposed a stretched-out version of the popular Viscount and a couple of new designs. American also was offered U.S. piston engine planes converted to turboprop engines. Douglas, as ever Lockheed's chief competitor, even then was busy on the DC-8 jetliner but still managed to come up with a new prop-jet transport proposal.

Lockheed jumped into the competition with a technical ace in the hole. It already had flown the C-130 Hercules, a muscular cargo plane designed for the Air Force and equipped with four 3750 horsepower Allison turboprop engines. The Burbank engineers designed an airframe for use with those well-tested power plants. American's equipment experts looked over all entries and picked the Lockheed color-bearer. So did Eastern.

Officially the new plane was assigned the unromantic

*DC-8*

sobriquet of L-188, *L* for Lockheed and the 188 standing for the project number. But Lockheed still had a penchant for naming its aircraft after stars.

"What do we call it?" a Lockheed official asked board chairman Robert Gross.

Gross, who for more than twenty years had nursed nostalgic sentiment for the trim little airliner that had saved his company from financial ruin, didn't hesitate one second.

"We'll call it the Electra," he said.

"It is," said Bob Gross to his engineers, "going to be the most thoroughly tested airliner in aviation history."

The engineers took him at his word. The Electra "flew" on drawing boards. In wind tunnels. On electronic computers. In laboratories. And in some of the most grueling flight tests ever to torture a commercial airliner.

They built three full-scale mock-ups, one structurally

complete fuselage section, layouts of complete systems, test rigs, engine stands, and a special sound chamber.

They constructed a full-sized wooden model to provide dimensional studies of passenger and flight-crew compartments, interior styling, and equipment location.

They fashioned a mock-up of metal for checking structural tolerance, fabricated parts, and actual operation of the complicated control systems.

They took a remote-controlled, stainless-steel ax and hacked away at a fuselage pressurized far beyond normal needs and subjected in advance to the simulated but violent turbulence of an approximate tornado—to determine if damage, once inflicted, could spread.

They slashed into window frames, windshield posts, skins and frames, door corners and fuselage-to-wing attachments.

They tore a six-foot gash in the fuselage and still couldn't make the wound spread.

"Fail-safe" structure was the aeronautical engineer's term. The providing of reserve strength so that if a major structural part failed, damage would remain localized and would not affect other key components.

They built a forty-foot unit that represented a regular Electra fuselage to check, test, and improve the heating and cooling system. It looked like a giant sausage because of its thick layers of insulating material placed around the tubing. But it manufactured weather on the ground and at 30,000 feet, and it made certain that the real airplane would remain comfortable at any level in any temperature.

They put twelve-inch samples of floor-covering material in the lobby of Lockheed's research laboratory. After 100,000 persons had walked over the samples, they picked the best.

They put a $48,000, one-sixteenth-scale model Electra through 60,000 wind-tunnel tests at speeds of more than 400 MPH.

They built two more scale models plus a reproduction of

the engine nacelles and flew each 100,000 miles to determine the Electra's aerodynamic characteristics.

They put the main landing gear through 270,000 simulated flights involving every load from an empty plane to one carrying ninety-five passengers plus full cargo and baggage bins and maximum fuel capacity.

They also put the gear through free-fall drop tests that duplicated the Electra's maximum sink speed of ten feet per second with a gross weight of 96,650 pounds. Then they pushed the weight up to 125,000 pounds—six tons heavier than the plane's greatest allowable take-off weight— and dropped the gear a few thousand more times.

They took four-pound carcasses of electrocuted chickens and blasted them out of a compressed-air cannon against cockpit windshields at 450 MPH. The chickens couldn't hurt the five-ply combination of glass and plastic, so they tried artificial hailstones and even steel pellets. Then they deliberately broke the outer glass and fired chickens, hail-

*Boeing 247*

stones, and pellets at the inner vinyl panel to see if it was strong enough to withstand any impact on its own.

They put the integrated staircase through 5000 cycles to see if it would break down or develop any bugs.

They loaded down the wings with sandbags, adding tons of weight gradually until they were sure they could withstand anything from an abrupt pull-out from a 400-MPH dive to the worst thunderstorm the heavens could create.

They put the wings on giant racks and subjected them to countless strains, twists, gusts, and violent maneuvers.

Allison technicians hurled frozen ice balls—make-believe hailstones—into engine air-intake ducts at speeds up to 415 MPH. They aimed a high-pressure stream of water into the engines to simulate the worst rainstorm any plane could encounter—the equivalent of 41.5 inches an hour, more than any recorded rainfall in history.

Lockheed already had accumulated 250,000 flight hours' experience with the Allison engines on the C-130s. But the engineers weren't satisfied. They mounted four of the big power plants on a Super Constellation and flew it for another 3370 hours.

In another Allison-equipped military transport, they conducted "Operation Hourglass"—twelve hours of flight daily over an airline type of schedule until the engines accumulated another 2000 hours.

When the Electra prototype finally was built, its various flight tests added 4200 more engine hours. Both ground and flight tests totaled 350,000 engine hours by the time the Electra was certificated.

As soon as the full-scale Electra mock-up was finished, complete to cockpit layout with full instrumentation, Lockheed invited aviation's severest critics to look it over—an evaluation committee from the Air Line Pilots Association, representing the flight crews of the several airlines that had ordered the plane by now.

The committee looked over the cockpit, the various systems, and the blueprints. It suggested sixty-three modifications, ranging from better fire-warning arrangements to the location of the cockpit ashtrays. Lockheed accepted thirty-nine recommendations, partially agreed to eighteen, and rejected only eight as impractical or unnecessary. It was the highest batting average for proposals accepted ever recorded by a pilot evaluation committee.

Later, committee members flew the actual plane. Two incidents of note occurred during the test program. One involved an accidental landing at a greater speed and with more forceful impact than encountered by a carrier-based fighter. There was only minor damage.

The ALPA evaluation report commented:

"The ability of the Electra to survive an impact . . . is remarkable and represents the best possible testimonial to its structural integrity."

In the second incident the test crew inadvertently kept the landing gear down for several minutes after taking off. The ALPA representatives were not even aware the gear was still down, because the Electra continued to climb without breathing hard.

Eighteen of the nation's best airline pilots were members of the committee. Their final report included these comments on the Electra's performance:

Landing—"the airplane had good control characteristics and no difficulty was experienced in making consistently good landings."

Emergency power during an aborted take-off—"members were very much impressed with the rapid power application possible and with the immediate airplane response in climb performance. It definitely exceeded the balked landing and pull-out of any propeller-driven airplane which we have ever flown."

Stalling—"the stall characteristics of this airplane, in all configurations, were exceptionally good. There was no fall-off on one wing or any other adverse tendencies. In fact, the stall characteristics were very similar to a 'Cub' with ample warning indication and no violent change of attitude."

Handling in the event of multiple engine failure—"the airplane is definitely flyable and controllable."

Stability—"high-speed stability is good . . . good control response at touchdown speeds . . . responded well to the flare-out on landing . . . cross-wind take-off and landing characteristics seemed to be most normal. . . ."

Cockpit visibility—"contrast between the visibility from the cockpit of the Electra and from previous Lockheed transports is tremendous. Visibility . . . is excellent and Lockheed is to be commended for the special effort that has been put into producing this cockpit."

Bad-weather landings—"in making ILS (Instrument Landing System) approaches, the airplane was found to be very easy to control on the glide slope . . . quite maneuverable and responsive and was considered by the pilots to be equal to or better than present-day transports in its handling characteristics."

The report concluded with about the most glowing praise ever offered in the traditionally conservative ALPA evaluation documents.

"This committee is more than reasonably confident," it declared, "that the manufacturers, the operators, the pilots and the public will be satisfied with the record of safety, efficiency and economy which will be achieved."

Typically, the ALPA evaluation report tempered praise with a sober note of caution.

"As has been true of all transports," it concluded, "the real evaluation of the Lockheed Electra will begin the day the first Electra airplane goes into scheduled airline operation and will continue until the last airplane of the final modification of the basic airplane has been retired."

That note of caution, however—that traditional touch of cynicism that is as much a part of the airline pilot as his uniform—was just an uneasy whisper amid loud acclaim for an airliner that seemed to have been conceived out of pilot dreams and desires. From the moment the first Electra snarled into the sky, it became the mistress, sweetheart, or wife of virtually every man who flew it. It was a ship that fulfilled the pilot's prerequisites for a transport better than any other plane in history. It had enormous reserve power. It handled smoothly, docilely, responsively. It was fast, versatile, uncomplaining, and even—for such a huge aircraft—forgiving of mistakes. In brief, it was a pilot's airplane.

The Electra's comparatively short, stubby wings bothered some pilots the first time they saw the plane. Captain Art Weidman, one of the first check pilots assigned to American's Electra training program, went out to the Burbank plant for his introduction to the new plane. Lockheed rolled out an Electra and Weidman's first question was:

"Where the hell is the wing?"

It was a natural question, for the wings do appear abnormally short. Actually the wing span is only five and a half feet shorter than the fuselage. Weidman was fooled by the size of the huge engines, with large exhaust nozzles extending to the trailing edge and literally hiding much of the wing area. The monster propellers also create the illusion of a "too-small" wing. But Weidman and other pilots quickly learned that Lockheed had built into the Electra a completely new airfoil.

American and Eastern had demanded a plane equally adept at short- and long-haul operations. This was achieved mostly by the thirteen-and-a-half-foot props, which swept their mighty air stream over all but nine feet of the wing area. The Electra was meant to manufacture her own lift in greater quantities than any plane ever built.

Demonstration flights proved to all doubting pilots that the engine-prop-wing combination resulted in fantastic performance. Weidman recalls one of those flights. Lockheed test pilot Herman "Fish" Salmon brought an Electra in for a landing, flaps partially extended, wheels down and locked. In every plane this is a moment of tension, for the pilot is committed to the touchdown. He can only wait for his aircraft to settle, then hit the brakes, reverse props, and come to a stop.

Salmon let the Electra's wheels touch the runway. Then, with an almost imperceptible throb of power, he suddenly began climbing again.

"I had never seen this done with any other aircraft in the years I had flown," Weidman marveled. "If I hadn't seen it with my own eyes, I wouldn't have believed it possible. This was the 'wave-off' characteristic that pilots had dreamed about but never enjoyed. An airplane that never really was committed to a landing. An airplane in which you could make as many passes at a field as you desired without any worry about emergency climb power."

Slim Cockes, a crusty and capable Eastern veteran, didn't believe what he heard about the Electra's effortless power until he took one off on a test hop at Miami's International Airport.

"When we passed over the runway threshold, we already were touching 3000 feet altitude," Cockes said. "The bird climbed like a damned fighter plane."

Lockheed spent 50,000 man-hours trying out more than one hundred flight-deck configurations. Of special interest and affection to pilots was the "panic button" for engine fires. All a pilot had to do was pull a single fire control lever. That one action automatically feathered the prop, shut off the fuel and oil supply, armed the chemical fire extinguisher and set it off. Emergency action time: one second. On a conventional plane the four separate procedures would take as long as ten seconds—which can seem like an eternity in an engine-fire situation.

The Electra's de-icing and anti-icing system works on the same single-motion principle. One push of a button and hot air is pumped from one of the engine's compressor stages. It flows instantly through stainless-steel ducts to the leading edges of the wings and stabilizers. It not only keeps ice from forming, but melts it in seconds. It is so efficient that it is possible to fry an egg on a wing edge being de-iced.

Lockheed extended much of the soundproofing in the cabin to the cockpit. The result was a flight-deck noise level that is about fifty percent quieter than a piston-engine cockpit and almost as quiet as the pure jets.

Even mechanics found they had been considered in the Electra's design. The plane squats relatively close to the ground, which means that many fuselage inspection plates can be opened without the necessity of a stepladder.

The anti-collision rotating light on most planes is on the top of the tail, requiring a crane or portable platform for changing. On the Electra there are two beacons located at the top and bottom of the fuselage. To replace the former, a mechanic needs only to unscrew it from inside the cabin. To change the bottom light, he just stands underneath the fuselage and reaches up.

Lockheed cut the overhaul time for props and engines by twenty hours, simply by using self-locking nuts and self-threaded inserts instead of the usual safety wire and cotter pins. Cabin-interior panels are pretrimmed and snap quickly in and out of place. A soiled or scratched panel can be replaced in a few moments.

The Electra also incorporated the hydraulically operated cabin stairs first introduced on the Convair 240. This was a design decision that appealed to the airlines, because an outside boarding ramp costs more than $3000.

Customer plaudits were not enough for Lockheed. The prototype Electra was sent on a round-the-world flight—the first such test program ever conducted for a commercial transport. It was no pleasure trip either. The test pilots deliberately went looking for rough weather. They slammed into thunderheads without slowing down. They landed on fields with runways about as smooth as a 4000-foot stretch of railroad ties. They flew in temperatures ranging from 40 below to 110 in the shade.

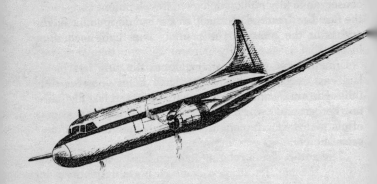

*Convair 240*

Before the Civil Aeronautics Administration (later to become the Federal Aviation Agency) certificated the plane as safe for carrying passengers, Lockheed subjected the Electra to tests the CAA didn't even require—abrupt pull-ups after deliberate high-speed dives. One such test was unexpected. The crew had a false fire warning and went into an emergency dive at a speed 100 MPH faster than any airline would ever fly the plane. When the fire-warning light suddenly flickered out, they pulled out of the dive—exerting a force on the wings greater than any CAA structural test.

Construction of the prototype began in December, 1955, with two firm orders on the books—thirty-five Electras for American and forty for Eastern. Later, a total of fourteen airlines ordered nearly 180 of the big planes. The first test flight came just two years later, on December 6, 1957, beating the Boeing 707's initial hop by two weeks and leaving the other two U.S. jet-age entries—Douglas and Convair—trailing by many months.

Behind that first flight were four years of research, a conservative fifty million dollars in development costs, and the firm conviction of Lockheed that it had designed, tested, and built the finest airplane in its long and honorable history.

Unfortunately, nowhere in the Electra blueprints—which, laid end to end, would stretch forty miles—nowhere in the reports of thousands of hours of ground and test flights—nowhere in 20,000 separate design studies or 7000 pages of mathematical calculations—was there any mention of a scientific phenomenon known as "whirl mode."

## 2

# "This Aircraft Trims Up Funny . . . ."

Aircraft N-9705C was the fifth Electra delivered of the nine Braniff had ordered.

At 10 P.M. September 29, 1959, ten days after delivery, it sat on a ramp at Houston, Texas, a $2.4 million symphony of aluminum, steel, and foam cushioning rendered temporarily inoperative by a three-hundred-dollar generator that had been acting up.

It was one of those minor mechanical gremlins that occasionally plague airliners, drive dispatchers crazy, cause passengers to complain, and set pilots to muttering, "I wonder who the hell designed the goddamned part."

The balky generator had nothing whatsoever to do with what was to happen to N-9705C. Mechanics fixed it by changing the voltage regulators on both the numbers three and four engines, twenty-eight passengers and six crew members boarded the plane, and N-9705C took off twenty-two minutes late as Flight 542, bound for New York International Airport with scheduled stops at Dallas and Washington, D.C.

At the very moment Flight 542 left the ground at 10:44 P.M., Lockheed Electras were busy compiling a proud and also profitable record. Nearly 100 delivered as of that date were carrying about 20,000 people daily in vibration-free comfort at speeds of more than 400 miles an hour. Passenger reaction to the roomy, well-upholstered cabins was

more than favorable. Airline officials also were pleased;
the Electra was the first transport in a long time that had
not only met but exceeded performance and operating-
economy specifications. Pilots were requesting Electra flights
even when the trips were at poor hours. About the only
occasional gripes heard were from those stewardesses who
didn't like the Electra's galley design. It was a complaint
that generally fell on deaf ears because of a commonly
held theory that no airliner galley ever built really satisfied a stewardess. It also was a commonly held theory on
the part of stewardesses that (1) all galleys were designed
as engineering afterthoughts and (2) no stewardess was
ever consulted until it was too late.

There had been a few operational bugs in the Electra.
Excessive vibration, felt mostly in the seats in line with
the four huge propellers, was the biggest problem. It was
typical of the illogical difficulties which, for some unknown
reason, do not appear in the thousands of hours of prototype test flights and invariably turn up only after a plane
has entered the rigors of regular airline service.

Lockheed's solution was simple, although expensive. It
changed the tilt of the engines, which in turn altered the
angle of the prop blades. Because airliners, like automo-
biles, have regular warranty periods, Lockheed had to foot
the seven-million-dollar bill for this comparatively minor
modification.

There were a few other early troubles, chief of which
involved reports of wing skin cracking—nettlesome but
actually about as dangerous to structural integrity as paint
chipping on an automobile fender. Some of these instances
were due to the vibration mentioned before. After Lockheed
corrected the vibration bug, two airlines operating Electras
found further skin cracks. These were traced to harder
than normal landings which transmitted the shocks from
the landing gear to a small wing area.

Lockheed put reinforcing straps over the affected
wing section and there were no other complaints. On

September 29, 1959, the Electra seemed well on its way to achieving both airline and passenger acceptance that rivaled even the popularity of the new jets.

True, there *had* been one fatal accident involving the new turboprop. It occurred on February 3, 1959, only twelve days after American inaugurated Electra service with understandable fanfare and justifiable pride (tempered slightly by the fact that Eastern had introduced its own Electras ten days earlier).

The captain of the ill-fated flight was a fifty-nine-year-old veteran named Albert Hunt DeWitt—only one year away from retirement and one of American's senior pilots, with more than seven million miles logged in 28,000 flight hours. On February 3 he was commanding Flight 320 from Chicago to New York's La Guardia Airport and was approaching Runway 22 in light rain and fog.

There was a subsequent welter of conflict, confusion, and controversy over what happened in the next few minutes. On one tragic fact, however, there was no dispute. Flight 320 ended in the chilling waters of the East River, nearly 5000 feet from the threshold of Runway 22. Of the sixty-eight passengers aboard—a full load—only five survived. DeWitt and a stewardess were killed. The copilot, flight engineer, and the other stewardess lived through the crash which, to this day, remains a classic example of an accident blamed on pilot error, but which also involved a number of booby traps that make an airman's own ultimate error almost inevitable.

DeWitt literally flew the Electra into the water, an unbelievable mistake for a pilot of his experience and skill. The Civil Aeronautics Board, in a report issued more than a year later, said the crew had neglected to monitor essential flight instruments—particularly those showing the plane's rate of descent and altitude. As far as his fellow American Airlines pilots were concerned, Al DeWitt and his unusually experienced copilot would have been more likely to have tried the landing blindfolded than to have ignored basic instruments during an instrument approach in bad weather.

The CAB did not agree, tagged the crew with "neglect of essential flight-instrument references," but cited a surprising number of contributing factors which in effect said 320 crashed because of mistakes made before, as well as during, the flight.

"The Board concludes there is no one factor so outstanding as to be considered the probable cause of this accident," the CAB report said. "On the contrary, the Board has found that the accident was an accumulation of several factors or errors which, together, compromised the safety of the flight."

The "factors or errors" which the CAB listed included the crew's limited experience with a new type of airplane (of DeWitt's 28,135 hours in the air, fewer than forty-nine had been spent in Electras), an erroneous altimeter setting, possible misinterpretation of a new type of altimeter radically different from the kind DeWitt had used for years, the fact that American had used conventional altimeters in training its Electra crews, the lack of adequate approach lights to Runway 22, and a pilot's sensory illusion of being higher than he actually is—a frequent source of trouble for crews making poor-weather approaches over water at night.

There also was indication that DeWitt's altimeter was faulty, although the CAB said it was hardly likely that the copilot's instrument was off too. At any rate, the new altimeters were removed from all Electras and the older, more familiar models installed. Nowhere in the CAB's report was there any criticism of the Electra itself. In truth, it was the kind of accident that had happened before and probably will happen again, so long as airports have inadequate approach lighting. Given proper visual facilities, whatever mistakes DeWitt and his copilot made in an instrument approach probably would not have been fatal ones. They would have seen modern approach lights soon enough to tell them they were too low.

The accident had no effect on the Electra's reputation, although there undoubtedly was some early uneasiness. Only twenty-two days elapsed between the start of Eastern's Electra service and the American crash. Never in commercial aviation history had there been such a short space of time between introduction of a new airliner and its first fatal accident. But the facts of the East River tragedy, obtained relatively soon, cleared the aircraft itself.

Between American's Flight 320 and Braniff's Flight 542 eight months later lay some 80,000 hours of generally trouble-free, uneventful Electra operations. Certainly there was no indication of impending disaster when 542 pointed her nose into the clear Texas night. Her four Allison engines with their distinctive low whine bespoke effortless, almost muted power.

It will never be known whether there was any sense of prophetic doom in a remark made by Dan Hollowell, 542's First Officer. He was a veteran pilot in his own right (more than 11,000 hours) who was flying copilot that night although he held a license to command—the coveted airline transport rating that gave him the right to wear the four stripes of captain.

Hollowell was conversing idly with an Allison representative while 542's voltage regulators were being changed.

"This aircraft trims up funny," Hollowell remarked.

There was no further discussion of that curious statement. In the subsequent investigation of 542's fate, the CAB found no mention of trim difficulties or peculiarities in N-9705C's logbook or any similar complaints by pilots who had flown her before September 29.

Gracefully, effortlessly, 542 reached its assigned cruising altitude of 15,000 feet exactly sixteen minutes after take-off. The time was 11 P.M. Second Officer Roland Longhill, the flight engineer, dutifully jotted down entries in his logbook.

Altitude 15,000. Airspeed 275 knots. Outside temperature 15 degrees. Anti-icing off.

At 11:05 P.M. the flight reported its position over Leona, Texas, as required, to San Antonio air traffic control.

"Roger 542," droned San Antonio. "Request you now monitor Fort Worth on a frequency of 120.8."

"542, roger," said Hollowell.

After switching to the new frequency, Hollowell next contacted Braniff's company radio at Dallas. The generators were working fine, he reported, but there had not been sufficient time in Houston to insulate a terminal strip on one propeller and the number 3 sump pump was inoperative. Both were minor items. Dallas said it figured the repair work could be done. It had no way of knowing that these two insignificant maintenance requests would be the last word heard from 542. In a sense, 542 had reported a couple of flea bites before it was to die of a monstrous metal malignancy.

Into Longhill's logbook went 542's epitaph.

"Transmission completed. 2307."

The time was 11:07 P.M.

Farmer White still was shoeless when he jumped into his small truck and raced down a dirt road toward Buffalo. There he found a state highway patrolman who picked up his cruiser microphone, calmly notified headquarters that an airliner was down, and then set off for the White farm with siren screaming.

In the next twenty-four hours a small army moved into the once peaceful world of the Richard Whites, where the most controversial item had been the right fertilizer for sweet potatoes and the only sound of death was the squawk of a hapless rabbit nailed by a hawk.

Through and beyond the Whites' potato patch moved the searchers. Their first object: the bodies of the twenty-eight passengers and six crew members. Their second: the wreckage in which those thirty-four persons had died.

Every last scrap of it, from the pulverized nose found in a crater four feet deep to a few tiny pieces of aluminum, plastic, and insulating material found nearly three miles away.

One of the earliest arrivals on the scene was a burly, dark-haired man named John Cyrocki—regional accident investigator for the Civil Aeronautics Board. Like most of his colleagues, he was an ex-pilot. Like all of his colleagues, he had long ago learned the prime lessons of accident investigation. No room for sentiment. No time for horror. No excuse for personal feelings—except the unspoken sickness that fills every airman's heart at the first unbelievable sight of plane wreckage, strewn about obscenely like the half-devoured carcass of a mighty beast that had seemed unconquerable.

Every CAB crash probe is carved from the same mold. Organization into teams. Each team assigned to one phase of inquiry. Each team composed of expert representatives from the groups with so much at stake in a final solution. The Air Line Pilots Association. The aircraft's manufacturer. The company that designed and made the engines. The Federal Aviation Agency, which cleared and guided the final flight and also is armed with awesome authority to order instant precautionary or corrective action based on even obscure, faint areas of suspicion. Finally, the airline itself.

Each party of interest, you might say, ready and willing to grind its own ax. ALPA to resist any verdict of pilot error. The manufacturers to clear their own products. The airline, which is the inevitable target for anger and recrimination from those who had the lives of husbands, wives, children, sweethearts, and friends snuffed out. Even the FAA to some extent, for its own rules and regulations or its standards for aircraft design may have played a role in the crash if they were in any way inadequate or obsolete.

Theoretically the CAB itself could have something of an ax to grind. It grants the certificates under which airlines operate, and there have been two fatal accidents involving non-scheduled airlines whose fitness to fly passengers was suspect.

Yet part of the residue of every crash is the need to fix responsibility for the accident. Not for the obvious legal reasons alone, but to prevent recurrence. At the head of each team is a CAB investigator—by experience, temperament, and inbred tenacity the theoretical personification of objectivity.

In a sense, he draws on the subjective zeal of the conflicting parties. He unites them in a common cause, knowing that they will seek the truth as he does, up to the point where their partiality may color interpretation of the truth. And such interpretation is the job of the CAB and no one else. The teams gather the evidence, unearth the clues, and produce the facts. Once this is accomplished, however, their role changes from active to passive and, like detectives who have suddenly become suspects, they must await the verdict of an agency that has no ax to grind.

This was the philosophy behind the investigation of Braniff Flight 542, as it was in the approximately 150 U.S. fatal airliner crashes that preceded it and as it will be in the accidents that follow it. Not all the verdicts were fair, just, and accurate. But the batting average for truth has been as high as anyone can expect, considering the ever-present margin for interpretive error, the human limitations of those involved, the frequent lack of solid evidence, and the absence of testimony from the only men who really know what happened in a fatal crash—the flight-deck crew.

Philosophical, however, was not the word for John Cyrocki's frame of mind as he organized the usual investigative teams—witness interrogation, structures, operations, systems, and engines. He had not been on the White farm for more than a few minutes when he got the chilling news. The left wing and its engines had been found a mile and a half from the potato patch where the bulk of the fuselage wreckage lay. And remnants of the right wing were spread along the flight path leading to the farm.

Mid-air disintegration? Sabotage? Structural failure from some unknown cause? The latter is an instant suspect in any catastrophic in-flight breakup of an airframe. But to Cyrocki and everyone else, the very possibility of structural failure was catastrophic in itself. This was a brand-new airliner, the proud product of every aeronautical test known to modern science, the legacy of all the research and progress that engineers had accomplished since the first metal transport was built more than three decades before.

The weather on September 30 was hot and sticky. The proprietor of the local feed store came out and sprayed the scene with a makeshift disinfectant, a conglomeration of insecticide and embalming fluid. A battalion of 300 soldiers from nearby Fort Hood arrived to aid in the search for wreckage. Cyrocki spread them out in a skirmish line a half mile wide and sent them through the chigger-infested woods bordering the White farm.

"Don't pick up any wreckage," he warned. "Just mark its location and keep going until you've found every scrap."

Most of what they found was in pieces not much bigger than a soup bowl. Approximately ninety percent of the forward fuselage, for example, was in crushed sections of two square feet or less. Two hundred feet away was the center section, fragments of the right wing, and what was left of the rear-cabin structure.

The cockpit was virtually unrecognizable. But searchers did find the flight engineer's log sheet. At 2300 (11 P.M.), he had recorded an indicated air speed of 275 knots—314 miles per hour, and with a tail wind, the plane probably was nudging 400 MPH.

At this point, the CAB knew only how fast 542 was going and how high it was just seven minutes before the unknown struck. It knew—again from the crumpled but still readable log—that engine and airfoil anti-icing systems were off and the outside temperature was 15 degrees above zero. Weather at the time of the accident was good, with partly cloudy skies. A check with pilots flying in the area before and after the crash turned up no reports of lightning, turbulence, or precipitation.

The witnesses team went to work contacting every known person who either heard 542 or saw it. The results were intriguing but also mystifying.

An engineer who had had some experience working jet power plants was driving home in his car when he saw a light flash in the sky. Like a phosphorus fireball, he recalled—first glowing, then subsiding, next flaring up and finally fading. But after the light, he heard a noise that he described as deafening. He could compare it only to the sound of a jet breaking the sound barrier.

Other witnesses told of the noise in descriptions that agreed on only one point: it was loud.

"The clapping of two boards together," said one.

"The sound of thunder," was another.

"The roar of a jet breaking the sound barrier."

"A whooshing, screaming noise."

"A creaking noise like a big bulldozer."

"Just an awful explosion."

Among numerous witnesses, the investigators found agreement on a curious phenomenon.

"When the sound came," said one farmer, "every coon dog for miles around started howling."

Interrogation revealed the truth of that observation. Every nearby farmer owning a hound reported that the animal began howling shortly after 11 P.M. It was a clue, although its significance was not clear.

The CAB went out and recorded twelve known noises of unusual intensity. Jet aircraft. Sonic booms. Propellers whirling at supersonic speeds. Electras in normal flight. Electras diving and climbing. Also intentionally random noises having not the remotest connection with an airplane or any part of one.

Cyrocki gathered the best of the witnesses and played the tapes for them individually. None was told the source of the noises. Each was asked to pick out the sound most like the one heard shortly after 11 P.M. on September 29. The witnesses picked two noises from the tape as coming the closest. One was that of a prop at supersonic speed. The other was the sound of a jet aircraft.

The structures team, meanwhile, was having its own troubles. There is no phase of accident investigation work that is more difficult, and some veterans of crash inquiries sadly commented they had never seen an aircraft in so many small pieces.

"I thought the Viscount that broke up over Maryland was pretty well mangled," one investigator remarked grimly, "but this was the worst I've ever seen."

*Viscount*

He was referring to a Capital plane ripped apart by a thunderstorm five months earlier. Actually, most totally fatal crashes look the same even to experts until they delve into the wreckage—a scattered pile of meaningless, twisted, scarred and scorched junk, heartbreaking in its awful finality and unbelievable to airmen, who take so much pride in their magnificent creations of metal and power.

The Braniff wreckage scene contained something even the veterans had never seen before at a crash—blood. There were obvious traces of blood all over farmer White's sweet-potato patch. Some news reports mentioned this item as delicately as possible, and to anyone fearful of flying it must have made a bad crash seem even worse. When the CAB got around to looking at flight 542's cargo manifest, however, it discovered a simple explanation. The plane was carrying a shipment of whole blood to a Dallas hospital. The containers had ruptured on impact.

Wreckage distribution was important, for it would show the pattern of what must have been mid-air disintegration. Air Force helicopters helped pinpoint locations. Bulldozers gouged out paths through the woods so the troops from Fort Hood could advance their search line. An Air Force photo reconnaissance plane was flown in from Langley Field, Virginia, to make over-all shots of the entire crash scene. This latter chore had to be done when a cloud cover disappeared, so the plane could fly high enough not only to take in the whole area, but to keep farmers from filing phony claims for "lost" livestock allegedly frightened by the noise (one of the minor hazards of air accident probes).

Some 'copters sweeping at treetop level over an area some distance from the nose crater found some puzzling pieces of aluminum foil. These, however, quickly were identified as chaff used in an Air Force radar training exercise. The foil, a World War II innovation, is designed to interfere with radar tracking of aircraft, but there was no possible connection with this accident.

Gradually the ground and air search parties located the severed jigsaw puzzle that had been a proud airliner. The wreckage at the nose crater consisted of the cockpit, some forward fuselage structure, and a few seats. Back in the direction from which flight 542 had come was the center cabin structure two hundred and twenty-five feet away.

Two hundred and thirty feet away were the tail cone, vertical fin and rudder, and the inboard stabilizers.

Seventeen hundred and sixty feet away was a large section of the right wing.

Two thousand and twenty feet away was the right stabilizer.

Four thousand and eighty feet away was the left stabilizer.

Fifty-three hundred feet away was the nacelle covering of the number four engine, known as QEC (for quick engine change).

Eighty-six hundred and forty feet away was the left wing, including the number four engine and number two QEC and propeller.

Ninety-nine hundred feet away was the number one propeller and gear box.

A full thirteen thousand, nine hundred feet away (2.3 nautical miles) was the last item located—a nine-inch section of hydraulic line that had been inside the number two fuel tank.

The engines on every plane are numbered from left to right. On a four-engine airliner, that means numbers one and two are on the left wing, three and four on the right. The various components of numbers one and two engines, plus sections of the left wing itself, were found the greatest distances from the nose crater. The entire wreckage pattern, allowing for the wind displacing some of the lighter pieces, was in a fairly straight line starting from about seventeen miles from the Leona VOR (the last radio check point) to the White farm. The first piece of the puzzle had slipped into place, just a tiny corner of a picture called Flight 542.

Structural failure of the left wing, then general disintegration.

This was not any complete answer, of course. There was the voluminous testimony from witnesses who had seen an apparent explosion, variously described as resembling a huge camera flash bulb or an electric welding arc, followed by a reddish-orange fireball. Did the wing fail because of an explosion or prolonged fire, or did the flash of fire result from igniting of fuel as it spewed from the ruptured wing?

The wreckage was taken to a Dallas warehouse, where the Structures Group began a mock-up, or reconstruction. The work went on steadily for twenty-six days—from October 12 to November 6. The reconstruction then was interrupted by a spate of aircraft accidents elsewhere that took several key CAB experts away from Dallas, much to the concern and annoyance of Braniff pilots working on the case. They did not blame the CAB, for to the ALPA participants it was another example of the Board's woefully understaffed Bureau of Safety being forced to spread itself too thin. (An aftermath of this and other crashes was a long-needed Congressional appropriation that allowed the Bureau to increase its investigators from 60 to 100.)

On November 23 Structures resumed the weary task of dipping into the two huge barrels jammed with tiny metal fragments and trying to fit them into larger pieces of wreckage.

The mock-ups of N-9705C, constructed under the supervision of CAB structures expert John Leak, were aimed mainly at determining whether fire preceded or followed the wing severance. As usual, it consisted of wood-and-chicken-wire frames on which fragments were placed in their correct relative positions. Contrary to popular belief, seldom is a mock-up assembled as a complete airplane, and those who see one are disappointed. They expect to view a reassembled aircraft that looks almost capable of flying again.

"Instead," Leak himself once commented, "what they see resembles an organized garbage collection."

But as in the past, this particular garbage collection yielded some valuable information in the sense that it eliminated possible suspects, even though it did not furnish the identity of the guilty party. The mock-ups were done in sections—one involving the fuselage, another the engine structure, a third the wings, and so on.

One of the theories being kicked around was a possible fire in the starter compressor, housed in the lower-rear fairing of the inboard engine nacelle. The compressor is driven hydraulically and has a magnesium case. When investigators pulled up the louvered cover panel, they found heavy soot streaks from the louvers that were typical of in-flight fire.

But during the mock-up, Leak fitted in the adjacent cover panel, which had not been subjected to any heat or fire. Engineers studied this area on an undamaged Electra and determined that any smoke exiting through the louvers had to flow over the interior of this adjacent panel. Leak concluded that the intense ground fire enveloping the magnesium case had forced smoke through the louvers at such high velocity that the smoke traces appeared similar to in-flight fire.

Leak also discovered that skin-panel fragments, when hung on the mock-up frame, were not burned in any reasonable pattern. One piece would be heavily sooted. The adjacent part would be completely clean.

The left rear side of the fuselage was covered with a fair amount of soot which was in both straight rearward and spiral patterns. No particular clue here, but the possibility of in-flight fire *prior* to breakup was raised again when laboratory tests on the rear windows showed they had been subjected to prolonged burning at intense temperatures. The heat had been sufficient to "craze" the Plexiglas and indicated longer exposure to flames than would have come from a flash fire produced by a wing fracture. But additional mock-up work explained this puzzler. It revealed that when the wing severed, the wing-to-fuselage fillet was exposed in the shape of a scoop—a freak distortion of metal that could hold and gradually feed out about forty gallons of kerosene. This had prolonged the invasion of fire on the rear fuselage.

In desperation, Leak and Cyrocki went back to the unlikely possibility of a tire blowout or even a hot wheel brake. Either might have ignited fuel or hydraulic fluid from broken lines in the wheel well. But the probers found the wheel-well door-actuating rods that had been thrown free of the ground fire area. They were as unmarked and clean as the day they came out of the factory.

By now it was definite that the fire had occurred after the wing broke off. The fracture itself was close to the fuselage and displayed evidence of strong twisting and yanking forces. But there was absolutely no sign of metal fatigue, no trace of any inherent structural weakness.

Sabotage was an early suspect but was discounted as soon as the fire damage was shown to have followed the breakup.

Could 542 have maneuvered violently to escape a collision? The FAA could not locate a single aircraft that had been anywhere near the Electra.

Could it have been trying to avoid a missile or could a missile have hit that left wing? Missile bases as far away as the eastern seaboard were checked. Nothing had been fired.

The CAB tracked down other possible but futile clues. An Eastern Electra had suffered some minor wing damage when excessive fuel tank pressure caused an overflow during fueling. Damage from such a source may appear farfetched, but an Electra's tanks can be gorged with 5500 gallons of kerosene in twenty minutes. Yet inspection of N-9705C's maintenance history disclosed no similar incident. Another Electra had experienced a small electrical fire near the wing roots, but there was not a shred of evidence that 542 had encountered anything like this. A third Electra had suffered a tire blowout in the air, causing damage to an engine nacelle. But nobody had ever heard of an exploding tire causing a wing to come off.

There was a great deal of speculation on the remark First Officer Hollowell had made just before the last takeoff from Houston—"This aircraft trims up funny." This suggested some kind of stabilizer or autopilot difficulty. But it also could have been the result of a slightly unbalanced fuel load, uncommon but not unknown. At any rate, the CAB never could trace the reason for Hollowell's comment, could find no indication of trim trouble, and for that matter wrote the remark off by pointing out that not a single crew member who had flown N-9705C during the ten days of its airline existence entered a trim complaint on the logbook. Besides, no two pilots trim an airplane in exactly the same way. What may seem like unsatisfactory trim to one may be perfectly acceptable to another.

At a fairly early stage of the investigation there was a widespread belief that the number two engine had caught fire, that the blaze could not be quenched, and that the flames eventually weakened the wing to such an extent that it failed. But this was belied by the Electra's superb fire-control system, one of the best ever designed. And again, the inspection of fire damage later knocked down this theory entirely, just as it knocked down any suspicion of sabotage. Furthermore, no engine fire in the history of commercial aviation ever had destroyed a plane in less than sixty seconds. There had been absolutely no emergency message from Flight 542. Fire would have been one item of serious trouble affording sufficient time for the crew to advise something was wrong.

How about the various noises witnesses had reported? Some had likened what they had heard to propellers whirling at supersonic speeds. This suggested the possibility of a runaway engine—and there had been solid evidence that the crew had feathered numbers three and four props. But these are on the right wing. It was the left wing that failed first. Besides, flight tests demonstrated beyond any doubt that an overspeeding engine caused no control difficulties with an Electra.

Some Lockheed engineers had a theory that a runaway prop going into supersonic speed without warning would have startled the crew to such an extent that the pilot flying the plane instinctively had reduced power and then yanked back on the controls to bring the nose up and reduce airspeed so abruptly that the wing failed. After all, this was an airplane relatively new to the crew, none of whom had any idea what a runaway prop-engine combination might sound like.

The theory didn't fit this particular crew, however. The captain of Flight 542, Wilson Elza Stone, was a forty-seven-year-old veteran of more than 20,000 logged flight hours. He had earned a long and enviable reputation of being positive yet smooth, demanding yet gentle, with every airplane he ever flew. The check pilot who rated Stone when he was transitioning to Electras remarked later that "he flew the Electra like he had written the operations manual himself."

For that matter, Lockheed itself admittedly was grasping at straws. It was too difficult to imagine how even a sharp pull-up at high speed could have torn a wing off.

This raised another question: could the plane somehow have plunged into a sudden, high-speed dive that resulted in the wing's separating when Stone tried to bring it out?

Lurking in every investigator's mind, like a nagging, uneasy conscience, was the phrase uttered by one farmer and backed up by so many of his neighbors: "Every coon dog for miles around started howling."

What kind of a sound frequency could have disturbed dogs in that way? Some engineers pointed out that in a dive surpassing 400 miles an hour an Electra's props would be whirling at supersonic speeds. One witness listening to those tape recordings had likened the sound to that of a supersonic prop.

But assuming the Electra had gone into an inadvertent dive, this would have involved some kind of control problem, and there was no evidence of any control malfunction. The elevator and aileron booster mechanisms were tested and found normal. The autopilot was too badly crushed for any tests, but even if this had engaged without warning and locked the controls in a dive position, it could have been disengaged immediately. Also the breakup, from a trajectory study of the wreckage distribution, indicated that structural failure began at the cruising altitude of 15,000 feet. (Further trajectory tests showed that failure also could have occurred at 5000 feet and resulted in the same wreckage pattern, but the lower altitude did not jibe with witness estimates of the fireball height.)

Three months after the crash, the CAB was unable to come up with the slightest inkling of a probable cause. On January 12, 1960, investigator-in-charge Cyrocki called a meeting of his investigative teams. He also invited representatives from the National Aeronautics and Space Administration, American, Eastern, the Army's Bureau of Aircraft Accident Research, and personnel from the Federal Aviation Agency's Los Angeles engineering division who, as employees of the CAA, the FAA's predecessor agency, had certificated the Electra. The meeting lasted five days, and one participant commented that "it looked like a re-evaluation of the whole Electra certification program."

Every component and system of the big prop-jet was discussed at length. Every conceivable weakness, failure, or malfunction that could have contributed to the accident, however remotely, was examined and debated. But no matter what possibility was brought up, eventually it was discarded.

"In every case," Captain G. K. Bruno of Braniff's own pilot investigating unit recalled, "the part or parts being

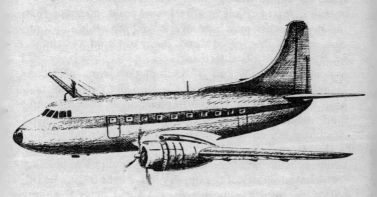

*Martin 202*

discussed were 'too strong,' 'too fail-safe,' or 'too inconsequential to contribute to the accident.' If the meeting had continued long enough, we all might have been convinced that the accident never happened."

Among the items mentioned was the condition of the number one propeller, which had separated from its engine. Damage marks revealed that it had been wobbling as much as thirty-five degrees from its normal plane of rotation prior to separation. No importance was attached to this, however. It was assumed that during the breakup of the left wing, the entire number one power-plant area had been subjected to unusually severe strains and stresses. The dedicated men hashing over the fate of Flight 542 could not have known that this was the crucial clue. It was in plain view, but its awful significance was masked by their innocent unawareness that an obscure theory of physics could tear the mighty Electra apart.

The following month, the CAB and Lockheed invited

experts from other aircraft manufacturers to study the wreckage in the Dallas warehouse. Perhaps a new look by outsiders might result in a fresh viewpoint, a chance that the investigators may have overlooked something in their closeness to the tragedy and their admitted weariness, frustration, and bewilderment.

Boeing, Convair, and NASA sent engineers to Dallas. Douglas wanted to participate but its key personnel had prior commitments. The visiting engineers looked, examined, debated, and discussed. They had some fresh theories but every one was checked out and discarded.

On March 8 the CAB held a pre-hearing conference just before opening what was billed as the final public hearing on technical phases of the inquiry into Flight 542. A Board official declared frankly that the CAB was ready to throw in the towel. ALPA's representatives objected strongly. So did spokesmen for Braniff management. The CAB relented and agreed to continue the probe.

Cyrocki got the Army to send a few hundred more troops into an unsearched area three miles south of the White farm. He hoped they might find some additional parts which might have fallen from N-9705C before the left wing failed. The soldiers found nothing. Braniff asked Captain Bruno to accompany management officials to Buffalo for the purpose of reinterviewing some witnesses. The company figured that some of the shyer, more cautious residents might be willing to come forth with new information if they thought the official phase of the inquiry was over. Several new witnesses were questioned, but what they saw or heard offered nothing helpful.

After six months of intensive but futile efforts, on March 17 the CAB was about to tell Braniff it could release the wreckage in the warehouse to its insurance underwriters— the final act of every accident investigation. It was a legalistic ritual that in ninety-six percent of previous crash inquiries had said in effect: "We have established a probable cause and we are through with the evidence."

This time the CAB apparently was through with the evidence even though it had not established a probable or even a possible cause. In no way can it be criticized. It had searched every crevice to no avail. There were no more avenues to explore, no more clues to examine, no more theories which remained to be checked out.

The CAB's dilemma was simple. It was faced with a single unpleasant fact. A wing had come off. It also was faced with numerous other facts, all of which said it was well-nigh impossible for that wing to come off.

Wing structural failure in modern airliners is rare. The metal transport dates back to the late 1920s. Since that time there have been only five cases of airliners losing wings—and four of them involved not structural weaknesses, but extreme turbulence which subjected the planes to violent maneuvers exceeding their design limits.

The fifth instance was the Martin 202, a twin-engine airliner introduced after World War II. In 1948 a North-

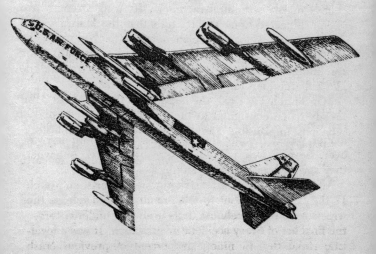

west Martin lost a wing in a thunderstorm over Winona, Minnesota, and crashed, killing all thirty-seven aboard. Other planes had flown through the same storm with no difficulty, however. Subsequently the CAB discovered that the 202's weakness was a key wing structural part built out of a new alloy. Supposedly strong, the part actually developed metal fatigue at a relatively early stage.

The CAB ordered immediate inspection of Northwest's seventeen Martins. Five had developed fatigue cracks and three of these had cracks in *both* wings. Every 202 then flying, and there were twenty-five of them either in service on various airlines or in the delivery process, was grounded for major wing modifications.

The Martin experience was a haunting memory to some CAB officials, who privately pondered recommending a similar grounding order for the Electra. Both ships had lost wings. But the cause of the 202's structural failure was spotted in less than two days. The Electra had no untried alloys in key structural members. Its wing strength had been subjected to far stricter tests than the Martin's.

There was no logical explanation for what had happened to Braniff Flight 542, no logical reason for suspecting anything was basically wrong with the Electra, and no logical argument for grounding it.

On March 17, 1960, the accident at Buffalo, Texas, was ready to be consigned to the unsolved category—one of the most implausible crashes in commercial aviation history.

But at 3:25 P.M. Central Standard Time on this St. Patrick's Day, another Electra lost a wing and plunged to earth near a small Indiana town called Tell City.

# 3

# Mirror Image

In midafternoon of March 17, 1960, the weather was clear over the flat farmlands of Indiana, except for scattered cumulus clouds. Thirty-one thousand feet above the partially snow-covered fields, three Air Force KC-135 tankers were busy wet-nursing three B-52 bombers on a refueling mission.

Not too far away, a Kentucky Air National Guard plane flown by Captain John Karibo, suddenly bounced like a car ramming a deep chuckhole at high speed. The force was so sudden and violent that Karibo was slammed against the canopy.

Clear-air turbulence, he thought—and a real lulu.

Karibo did not know it at the time, but he was lucky. At 18,000 feet, a four-engine airliner was approaching Tell City, Indiana, at more than 400 miles an hour. Perhaps the sixty-three persons aboard were fortunate in a way, too. Mercifully, they did not know that death was only seconds away.

Somewhere in that deceptively peaceful sky lurked the unseen killer known as clear-air turbulence. It grabbed more than 105,000 pounds of aircraft like a giant fist and twisted.

Two puffs of white smoke blossomed. Then a large cloud of ugly black smoke.

Two loud explosions split the sky, causing startled farmers to look up.

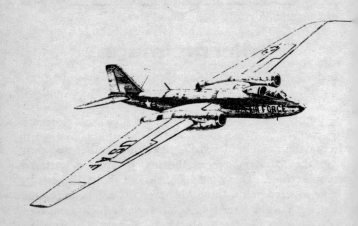

*RB-57*

The airliner's fuselage emerged from the black cloud minus its entire right wing and with only a large stub of the left wing still attached. For a few seconds it continued in level flight, in brave defiance of the relentless law of gravity. Then it began an almost vertical plunge to earth, trailing smoke and fire like a spent rocket.

Down it came, throwing off smaller metal objects in its arching trajectory.

It struck a soybean field at 618 miles an hour. Mud, dirt, grass, shrubs, and mottled snow were tossed two hundred and fifty feet in the air. The debris fell back around a muddy crater forty feet wide. From this gaping wound in the earth poured smoldering smoke. There were pieces of wreckage around the perfectly formed rim. Some other metal fragments were hurled fifteen hundred feet away. But the one-hundred-foot fuselage itself had disappeared entirely.

In the crater, buried twelve feet under this smoking

devil's caldron, was what was left of Northwest Airlines Flight 710—and the thirty-three men, twenty-one women, and eight children and one infant aboard.

Flight 710 was bound from Minneapolis to Miami with a single scheduled stop at Chicago's Midway Airport. Its equipment on this particular day was Northwest's very first Electra, N-122US, delivered to the airline the previous July. It had less than 1800 flight hours logged and only a week earlier it had gone through a major inspection.

Flight 710's captain was fifty-seven-year-old Edgar E. LaParle, a heavy-set, jovial man known throughout Northwest for his love of good food. LaParle enjoyed eating. He also enjoyed flying. He must have. He had joined Northwest in 1937, and his logbook showed a whopping 27,523 hours. And as was the case with many NWA captains, they were not easy hours. Northwest's original routes involved some pretty rugged country and weather. It is an airline axiom that you can spot a Northwest pilot by the crow's-feet around his eyes—and also judge his flight experience by them, as you tell a tree's age by the rings.

When you were introduced to Ed LaParle, his first act was the conventional handshake and his second invariably was to pull out his pilot's certificate.

"Take a look at the number," he'd say proudly. "Two-seventy-five. Don't see many that low."

His pride in his early license was typical of a man whose entire life had been connected with flying. Both his parents had been pilots. He had something of a potbelly and he didn't really look like the Hollywood version of an airline captain. But he could fly an airplane and he had stared death squarely in the eyes on many occasions without flinching. Like many old-timers, he had come to the grudging realization that the younger men coming up were just as good and perhaps better in their technical grasp of the more intricate equipment that was their job.

When LaParle decided to bid Electra trips, he openly

admitted "It's just to show you young guys an old warhorse can handle these new birds."

A Northwest pilot colleague recalls that LaParle hit the books during his Electra transition course "like a rookie whose very job depended on not just a passing grade, but the best showing possible."

"He said at the time," the pilot related, "that he felt the veterans were on trial with a new ship like the Electra."

Flight 710's copilot was pleasant, serious-minded Joseph Mills, who had no aversion to Electras but really was in love with another plane—the old Boeing 377 known as the Stratocruiser. Northwest had traded in its Boeings for the airline's nine Electras, much to Mills's unhappiness. He had flown the military version of the Stratocruiser while in the Air Force and would tell anyone willing to listen that the fat, clumsy-looking Boeings were the best airplane ever built. But he also was only twenty-seven, ambitious, eager to earn his coveted four stripes as a captain, and he

*Boeing 377 Stratocruiser*

was secretly proud to fly copilot on the new queen of Northwest's fleet even while he was bewailing the fact that Northwest had scrapped the Stratocruisers.

Then there was the rest of Flight 710's crew. Cautious, meticulous, sad-eyed Arnie Kowal, the flight engineer. Flight attendant Mitch Foster, who wasn't supposed to be on 710 but had traded trips with a colleague as a personal favor. The same was true for one of the two stewardesses. (More than a year later the girl whose place she had taken again traded a flight, and that flight also ended in a fatal crash; the young lady resigned the next day.)

To a competent crew, the Minneapolis-Chicago-Miami schedule was a comparative milk run. Particularly to LaParle, who had cut his pilot's teeth on Alaskan storms and looked forward, along with his mates, to the one-night layover in sunny Florida. It was in a happy frame of mind that he waved to the ramp personnel at Wold-Chamberlain Field in Minneapolis, wheeled the red-tailed Electra toward its assigned runway, and waited for Joe Mills to give him the tower's take-off clearance.

The Minneapolis-Chicago segment was covered in one hour and four minutes. Ostensibly the landing was routine, but subsequent events led the Civil Aeronautics Board to question closely the passengers who deplaned at Midway. Some claimed the landing was very hard. Yet others said it seemed completely normal. Such conclusions admittedly are indefinite. The average passenger is not a trained critic of flying technique, and the knowledge of what eventually happened to Flight 710 may have influenced at least some of the "very hard landing" opinions. On the other hand, there was one Electra landing so rough that the gear was damaged—and not a single passenger felt anything out of the ordinary.

N-121US was on the ground at Midway for a half hour. Captain LaParle, during refueling operations, went to the Northwest operations office, where he reviewed the latest weather information for the Chicago-Miami portion of the flight. The forecast did not mention the possibility of clear-air turbulence along the route. More than a year later, the CAB's report on the Tell City accident would criticize the U. S. Weather Bureau and Northwest's own meteorology department for not giving LaParle a warning based on the presence of turbulence-creating conditions and numerous pilot reports that severe or even extreme clear-air turbulence was most likely on 710's path southward.

N-121US's wheels left the ground for the last time at 2:38 P.M. Seven minutes later, Flight 710 reported to the Air Route Traffic Control Center at Indianapolis it was over Milford, Illinois, at 18,000 feet and estimating Scotland, Indiana, the next radio check point, at 3:12 P.M. The estimate was one minute off. At 3:13 the flight reported over Scotland, "maintaining 18,000 and estimating Bowling Green [Kentucky] at 1535," or 3:35 P.M.

ARTC advised 710 to contact the Memphis, Tennessee, ARTC Center on 124.6 megacycles at 3:50 P.M.

"Acknowledged," said 710. It was the last message received.

Radar at the Indianapolis Air Surveillance Station monitored 710 as far as Scotland. The tracking showed a normal, steady path.

At 3:32 P.M., seven minutes after 710 slammed into the ground, the six Air Force jets on the refueling mission first noticed a strange smoke trail. It was the shape of a child's top and dark in color. It reached a height of 25,000 feet and showed no sign of dissipating.

At 4:40 P.M. Indiana state police notified Northwest that one of its planes had crashed near Tell City. No survivors.

At 5 P.M. a ticket agent at Northwest's counter at Miami International Airport, lips tight and eyes somber, chalked a single word on the arrivals board next to the lettering: "Flight 710, Due 6:21."

"Canceled," was the word he wrote.

\*     \*     \*

An air crash involving total destruction often leaves behind some weird and poignant residue. Such as perfectly tied shoes, resting forlornly as if they were in a store window waiting for a customer to try them on. Or an operations manual, flipped open to a page on how to operate storm-warning radar—this one found in a plane that had crashed in a thunderstorm because its radar was inoperative.

But the residue from Flight 710 was something even the most veteran investigators had never come across before. There were no bodies.

Newsmen arriving on the scene quickly noticed that shirts, towels, women's slips, and other items of clothing were hanging from nearby trees. Quite naturally they phoned in the gory news that the clothes had been stripped from the victims' bodies by the explosive impact. Like the blood incident at Buffalo, their observation was accurate but their analysis faulty. The items draped on the tree branches were from a bale of old clothing that Northwest was shipping to its maintenance shop in Miami for grease rags. When impact burst open the baggage compartment, the assorted clothing was flung into the air and fluttered down among the trees.

Where *were* the victims? Masked workers wearing plastic gloves dug into the smoking crater. They dug down a full twelve feet before they found what they were seeking. The huge fuselage had telescoped and compressed into a mass of molten metal only one third its original length. Of the sixty-three occupants, there was not enough left to identify—eventually—more than seven bodies. The aluminum fuselage that was their coffin was so hot that five days later a steam shovel picked up pieces that still were burning.

The crater itself measured forty feet from north to south and thirty feet from east to west. The contents were so sickening that even the most hardened turned away in horror.

An army chaplain from nearby Fort Knox bluntly urged

that bulldozers be brought in to cover up the entire crater area—wreckage and all.

"In the name of humanity," he pleaded eloquently, "mark the spot to prevent desecration but leave the bodies there!"

But the CAB also had a duty to humanity—that portion which entrusted their lives to the great metal birds of commerce.

The local coroner, under mounting pressure from health authorities, sided with the chaplain. Even some Northwest officials momentarily weakened and said they would not object. It was as if they thought covering up the crater could blot out the very fact of the crash itself from all memory.

The coroner announced he would call in the bulldozers. The CAB went swiftly to the Governor of Indiana and obtained an official order preventing the coroner from going ahead. To the CAB, its duty was only too clear: the product of a nation's aeronautical genius had become a double killer, and the CAB had to find out why.

Three hundred and fifty soldiers from Fort Knox, supported by the ubiquitous helicopters, walked slowly forward in a wide skirmish line into a twenty-five-square-mile area. They were followed by members of the CAB investigating teams who marked, identified, and plotted each piece found. The right wing was located eleven thousand, two hundred and ninety-one feet from the crater. The mirror image of Buffalo had begun to form.

Inevitably some of the early arrivals at the scene were congressmen, giving forth with some understandable statements of concern and some uninformed opinions of what caused the accident.

"One of them," recalls an FAA official whose name for obvious reasons shall forever remain this writer's secret, "walked up to the rim of the crater, stood there for a few minutes, and announced that propeller metal fatigue was responsible! Hell, at that point we hadn't even found the props."

But the presence of alarmed lawmakers was indicative of more than the usual politician's propensity for getting into the act. Not three hours after the crash there were rumors that the Electra was to be grounded.

In less than twenty-four hours the CAB Witness Group had garnered much more solid evidence of what had happened to Flight 710 than interrogators had been able to unearth in the early stages of the Buffalo crash.

Captain Karibo, the RB-75 pilot who had encountered spine-jolting turbulence in the same area, came forth quickly to report his experience.

"There was sort of washboard roughness at first," he related, "then bang!—a chuckhole."

Colonel Daniel Shea, another Air Force pilot, recounted how his T-33 jet trainer had rammed into clear-air turbulence so severe that he was tossed out of his seat.

A swift check of the Weather Bureau revealed that atmospheric conditions conducive to extreme turbulence were very much present on March 17. The jet stream at 18,000 feet, the CAB was told, was in excess of one hundred miles an hour and aimed at a ninety-degree angle to Flight 710's path. Horizontal and vertical wind shears of huge magnitude was the technical phraseology. The brutal, twisting hands of an invisible giant was the non-technical way of putting it.

It was obvious that Flight 710, boring a hole through the sky at more than 400 miles an hour, had bounced into an aerial ditch—a jarring collision of metal and wind in which the metal had come off second best.

But clear-air turbulence had been around since planes able to reach the high altitudes where it lurks were built. The phenomenon had never wrecked a plane before. Why the Electra—an aircraft of brute strength that not only met but exceeded the structural standards set by the federal government itself?

At this point a considerable number of persons—pilots, engineers, CAB investigators and congressmen—were convinced something was wrong with the Electra serious enough to warrant its temporary removal from passenger service. But the only government official with such drastic authority was the head of the Federal Aviation Agency. And at this point there arrived at Tell City the stocky, rosy-cheeked, trigger-tempered former Air Force general who had headed FAA since its inception—Elwood R. Quesada.

# 4

# "If Another One Goes Down . . ."

He was not, by a long shot, the most popular government official in the Eisenhower administration. In his two years as FAA chief he had feuded with pilots, put the fear of God into subordinates, antagonized the airlines, and with few exceptions had united some widely diversified segments of the aviation community into their first unanimous opinion: Pete Quesada was an arbitrary, unreasonable autocrat.

In his military flying days, Quesada had been a hot fighter pilot with many of the carefree characteristics that go into the make-up of a hot fighter pilot. Even as a general he was somewhat informal and unorthodox, occasionally winking at regulations, rules, and procedures. Such transgressions were considered completely normal.

Both in civil and military aviation, the commander of a large aircraft has more than just himself to think about. The protocol of a royal court is adhered to no less rigidly and unquestioningly than the operational rules of multi-engine airplanes. But fighter pilots by instinct, training, and philosophy are the lone wolves of flight.

Pete Quesada was no exception. True to his breed, he was something of a maverick—which made his administration of the new Federal Aviation Agency seem more startling by contrast. It was not unlike having a juvenile delinquent suddenly appointed to the police department and turning out to be one hell of a tough cop.

The new agency, and for that matter all civil aviation, needed a tough cop. Enforcement of civil air regulations had grown slack under the politically harassed, money-starved old Civil Aeronautics Administration. Given a clean broom and almost unlimited authority, Quesada proceeded to use the broom not only for cleaning but spanking purposes, and he was impartial in his choice of targets. Violation reports filed against airlines and their crews, business and private pilots, and manufacturers mushroomed to unprecedented proportions.

Like so many reformers who are handed what amounts to a blank check of authority, Quesada demonstrated one weakness. He assumed for himself and his powerful new agency virtually the sole judgment of right and wrong as applied to air safety. He more often than not was right. He also could be, as his critics charged, unreasonable, arbitrary, and very wrong. His fast-flailing broom sometimes swept out the good along with the bad, went into corners that didn't really need cleaning while ignoring corners that did, and slapped the innocent along with the guilty. Several years later, when Quesada had long since retired from government to run the Washington Senators baseball team, a special task force appointed by Najeeb F. Halaby, his successor, sharply criticized many of FAA's enforcement procedures as unfair. It conceded that those procedures largely stemmed from the sense of urgency that had brought a more powerful air agency into being after years of neglect and indifference toward air safety. But it also remarked that no court felt capable of throwing out a government action taken in the name of safety, even if the action was unwise.

Quesada's zeal was combined with all the faults and virtues of his military mind. He was ruthless, demanding, and impatient. He also was courageous, frank, and completely honest in his convictions. It was typical of him that

he thought the FAA and not the CAB should investigate
air accidents. It apparently never occurred to him that the
FAA in some accidents may well be a defendant, with its
own rules, regulations, procedures, and personnel under
suspicion. He merely assumed that any responsible agency
could assume blame as well as attach it, just as the military
itself administers its own internal justice.

In brief, Pete Quesada was both feared and respected—
hated, yet grudgingly admired. For while his long military
career had imbued him with some of the unpleasant quali-
ties of an autocrat, it also had imbued him with a magnificent sense of unyielding devotion to duty. He sincerely
and deeply felt that his obligation was not to airlines or
pilots or manufacturers or even Congress, but to the public. Rightly or wrongly, everything he did as FAA chief
was in the name of the public, its welfare, its safety, and
its interest.

Inasmuch as being for the public's safety was like standing foursquare against sin, it was hard to question his
actions and almost impossible to overrule them. Quesada
literally put his opponents in the untenable position of
being against safety every time they tried to fight him.

It was this creed of duty, this sometimes too rigidly
applied sense of responsibility, that in the day-to-day operations of the FAA led Quesada into command decisions
that might better have been exposed to consultation or, at
times, even compromise. But it was a quality ideally adapted
to a major emergency requiring swift decisions unfettered
by fear or uncertainty.

And on March 17, 1960, the Lockheed Electra had
become a very real emergency—one affecting not only the
airlines that flew the prop-jet and its manufacturer, not
only its crews and trusting passengers, but the entire
aviation community. The day after the crash Pete Quesada
walked over to the lip of the smoking crater and looked
down on a few square feet of death and disaster that could
become his own grave as a public servant. Gone was the

deceptively perpetual smile that creased his ruddy, pleasant face even when he was angry. But there was no time for pity and even less time for indecision.

From one of his own officials, square-jawed Joseph Hornsby of FAA's Compliance and Evaluation Section, came an early suggestion. If the Electra was not to be grounded, put it under speed restrictions.

"The pilots have been flying it right up to the red line," Hornsby pointed out. "We know that the Northwest plane hit turbulence at high speed. If we slowed the plane down, we'd be adding a considerable safety factor and eliminating at least one major danger."

In the back of Hornsby's mind lurked the one element of doubt about the Electra that existed among many airmen. True, it had passed every structural test required by the government. But it happened to be the fastest propeller-driven airliner ever to fly. It was taking its conventional, straight wings into speed areas not far away from those of the forthcoming pure jets, who their swept-back wings designed to absorb subsonic turbulence.

Hornsby, a pilot himself, was well aware of how difficult it is to slow down a fast-flying aircraft in a hurry—and clear-air turbulence gives no warning at all. By placing speed restrictions on the Electra, he argued, in effect it would be adding strength to its wings. Almost at the same time, Lockheed officials approached Quesada with the same proposal.

The first FAA order involving the Electra went out three days after Tell City. All pilots were forbidden to fly the plane faster than 275 knots. Admittedly it was a temporary move, and Northwest Captain Robert N. Rockwell, a member of the NWA-ALPA accident-investigating team, promptly reminded FAA that 275 knots was the speed which the Braniff plane was making when it began to break up.

The 275-knot figure had been established after some hasty calculations by Quesada and by Oscar Bakke, a soft-spoken man who was then his Director of Flight Standards, and who had once headed the CAB's Bureau of Safety. Quesada admitted that it was not a totally satisfactory precaution, and a whole platoon of FAA experts, working with Lockheed, were in the midst of determining a truly safe speed limit.

Actually the FAA could have slowed the Electra to the speed of an ancient Ford trimotor and it would have done little to quell the rising demand for total grounding. Some CAB officials returning to Washington from Tell City refused to travel in an Electra—a fact withheld from the press. If this had leaked out, there would have been no need for a grounding order; the airlines could not have paid people to fly in an Electra.

At Tell City investigators packed what remained of N-121US into crates and shipped them to Burbank. The engines went to the Allison plant in Indianapolis. The same was done at the Dallas warehouse with the Braniff wreckage. The CAB had decided to combine both accidents into a single inquiry.

Senator Vance Hartke of Indiana phoned Quesada.

"I assume you're going to ground the Electra," he said bluntly.

"No, I'm not," Quesada snapped.

Angered, Hartke reminded the FAA chief that if another Electra went down, it would be Quesada's responsibility.

"I'll accept that responsibility, Senator," Quesada replied firmly.

The pressure for grounding was coming from more directions than just Capitol Hill, however. Edward Slattery, veteran press officer of CAB's Bureau of Safety, took the unprecedented step of asking permission to appear before the full five-man Board, urging grounding.

Slattery, a graying, burly man who had been crippled by a bone disease since childhood and could walk only on crutches, had been a part of CAB accident investigations for years. What he had seen at Tell City had burned into his mind, heart, and soul. Fervently and eloquently he pleaded his case.

No civil aircraft to which passengers entrust their lives should be allowed to fly with what obviously was some unknown structural deficiency, he argued. Two Electras had lost wings in level flight, one of them in calm weather with no turbulence. Until the reason was found, the Electra must be grounded or it could happen again. And if it happened a third time, he reminded the solemn-faced Board, the Electra would be ruined forever, its reputation smashed far beyond what a grounding order could do.

There was precedent for the CAB's recommending grounding, he went on. The Martin 202, also victim of structural failure, was taken out of the skies only twenty hours after the Winona, Minnesota, crash. The DC-6 had once been grounded, and for a lot less serious weakness than the Electra evidently—a poorly placed air scoop that could suck fuel into the heating system if a pilot allowed a wing tank to overflow during a fuel transfer from one tank to another. So had the Constellation, because of another fire-causing weakness in the electrical system.

Of course it had hurt the airlines when these three fine ships were grounded, Slattery conceded. Schedules were wrecked and thousands of dollars lost. But better a wrecked schedule than the possibility of another wrecked airplane. For that matter, he continued, financially speaking this was the most opportune time Electra operators ever would have to pull their new prop-jets out of service until Buffalo and Tell City were solved. They still had plenty of older DC-6s, DC-7s, and Constellations to operate their schedules even if their Electras were grounded.

Northwest, he pointed out, could recall the nine Boeing Stratocruisers it had turned over to Lockheed as trade-ins on the Electras. American had plenty of DC-7s. Eastern had a sizable fleet of Constellations, and so on.

One of his key arguments was that a precedent had

*DC-7*

been set for helping the airlines recover some of the losses
suffered because of grounding. In 1946, when United and
American jointly agreed to take their DC-6s out of service
until the location of the air scoop was changed, the CAB
recognized that the new Douglas plane was serving the
two carriers' most lucrative long-range routes. Grounding
meant substitution of the 230-mile-an-hour DC-4 for their
300-mile-an-hour queens, and the DC-4s were not only
smaller but also unpressurized.

United's and American's DC-6 fleets stayed on the ground
for nearly six months, at a cost of about eight million
dollars in lost revenues. The CAB awarded them more
than two million dollars apiece in federal subsidies. Slattery
felt that the Board might well be willing to consider the
same aid for Electra operators.

Ground the Electra, he urged, until its Achilles' heel
was discovered. Ground it before another crash ruined it
as an airliner for all time. Ground it before another crash

destroyed not only the plane itself but the public's faith and trust in the two federal air agencies supposedly guarding its safety.

Grounding, he continued, could not hurt the Electra any more than it already had been hurt. Keeping it out of the air until Buffalo and Tell City were explained and the faults corrected was, in the long run, the best way and the only way to restore public confidence in the plane.

"Therefore," he concluded in a soft but forceful voice threaded with his noticeable Boston accent, "I respectfully urge that the Board recommend unanimously to the FAA that the Electra be grounded."

The Board took no immediate action. But on March 23 Quesada summoned all Electra operators to a closed-door meeting at FAA headquarters. The announced general topic: the Electra. The unannounced subject that everyone knew would be discussed: should it be grounded?

The meeting was held in a large room that had once been the patients' solarium of the old Washington Emergency Hospital—the only building the new air agency had been able to acquire in space-short Washington. A current crack was that Quesada's office had once been the operating room, but this was too good to be true.

Sunlight, bright and cheery, streamed incongruously into a room filled with grimness.

Present were either the presidents or vice-presidents of every U.S. carrier flying Electras. Also there were representatives of Allison; the Navy, which was operating an antisubmarine version of the prop-jet; the Australian Embassy, speaking for a "down-under" airline that had bought the plane; the full Civil Aeronautics Board; and Robert Gross, Lockheed's husky board chairman.

An able FAA public information official, Chet Spurgeon, checked in each person. Big C. R. Smith of American. Tough old Eddie Rickenbacker of Eastern. Handsome Don Nyrop of Northwest, himself a former CAB member. Quesada had told Spurgeon not to let anyone in who was not a current operator of the Electra. Spurgeon, following orders explicitly, banned the chief pilot of the South American airline, Avianca. The carrier had ordered three Electras and was about to take delivery the very next day, but the chief pilot was refused admittance.

Quesada personally ejected another would-be participant, an attorney who represented one of the operators but did not actually work for it. Quesada, standing at the door with Spurgeon, spotted the lawyer and immediately challenged him.

The lawyer said he was with Blank Airlines. Quesada demanded to know if he was *with* the airline or just representing it. The lawyer acknowledged he was not a bona fide employee of the carrier.

"Out!" said Quesada curtly, waving his thumb like an umpire dismissing an overargumentative baseball player.

The doors were closed and locked. Quesada declared that no minutes were to be taken and asked Spurgeon if he was sure there were no members of the press present. Spurgeon said he was.

[The following account is based on interviews with principals who were present.]

Quesada then opened the fateful session by stressing that this would be an informal discussion of the Electra situation, what the FAA intended to do about it, and how the operators, Lockheed, Allison, and the CAB felt about it. He said there were no reporters present and that all might speak freely. He emphasized that he wanted to hear their views and that he would respect them. But whatever action would be taken, the responsibility would be his.

He announced that he had requested and would receive the technical assistance of the National Aeronautics and Space Administration, which would put its wind tunnels at Lockheed's disposal. He then revealed the orders FAA was about to put into effect.

Further reduction of Electra operating speeds to 259

miles per hour, taking it below the 315-MPH, or 275-knot, limit that the pilots had warned was too high.

All Electra autopilots were to be deactivated until it was proved the autopilot had played no role in the two accidents.

All operators were to follow to the letter Lockheed's recommended fueling procedures.

FAA inspectors were to make thorough structural checks of all Electra wings.

Daily inspections would be made of the engine reduction gears (which keep the propeller from spinning as fast as the turbines).

Any Electra which had gone through severe turbulence or experienced a hard landing would have to be given a complete structural inspection before being allowed to resume flying.

Airlines would make sure that pilots were advised of the new speed restrictions and that they were following all flight techniques and procedures contained in Electra operating manuals.

At the earliest possible date, impact-immune flight recorders, which depict on tape an aircraft's speed, course, altitude, elapsed time, and the G forces encountered, were to be installed on every Electra.

Lockheed was to undertake a program of engineering research and experiments so vast in scope that it amounted to a complete reevaluation of the plane.

That, Quesada concluded, was what the FAA intended doing about the Electra. Any questions or comment?

Big Bill Littlewood, American's vice-president for equipment research, arose and read a formal statement defending the Electra and backing the FAA's decision not to ground it. Quesada was openly irked, not at the contents, but at the fact that they had been prepared in advance. He snapped a reminder that the meeting was informal.

Gross of Lockheed lurched wearily to his feet, his normally jovial face showing the terrible strain of recent events. Quietly he described the flight tests Lockheed had started that very day in fully instrumented Electras. The company, he added, also would test an Electra's wing to the point of destruction. Lockheed was calling back a Northwest Electra with approximately the same number of hours as the Tell City plane, and this would be tested for any unsuspected weaknesses that might be occurring at a particular point in a plane's life span. Lockheed, he declared, did not feel grounding was necessary, because the reduced speed limits and inspection program furnished an unusual margin of safety.

Quesada asked CAB chairman James Durfee if he had anything to say. Durfee, blithely ignoring Quesada's nettled comments on Bill Littlewood's prepared-in-advance remarks, sailed into a formal statement of his own. Speaking for the Board, he urged that grounding be considered and repeated the arguments Slattery had cited before the CAB itself.

When Durfee finished, the room erupted into a flurry of airline brass clamoring for the floor. Quesada recognized Nyrop of Northwest. The meeting hushed as the usually brisk and brusque head of NWA clenched the seat in front of him and began speaking, quietly but with undisguised emotion.

Only a few days before, he had asked Lockheed to return the Stratocruisers Northwest had traded in on its Electras. It had been apparent that he expected a grounding order. Now he was to make it clear he wanted one. He was almost in tears as he told his fellow airmen that regardless of what the others did, Northwest's Electras would be grounded by the end of the day.

A roar of protest greeted the white-faced Nyrop. Rickenbacker, blunt-talking hero of World War I and probably the most colorful, controversial airline executive in the world, proclaimed angrily that Eastern would continue to fly its Electras. C. R. Smith, whose own colorful personality was only a shade lighter than Captain Eddie's, put American side by side with Eastern.

Several of Nyrop's colleagues figuratively jumped down his throat, warning him that if Northwest grounded its prop-jet fleet, the other carriers would be forced to follow suit, that it would be impossible to explain to the public why one airline grounds the plane and the others won't.

[Author's Note: It must be mentioned at this point that when the writer interviewed Nyrop two years later, he denied ever favoring grounding. Yet Quesada and several others present at the March 23 meeting insisted that Nyrop not only wanted to ground the Electra but promised that Northwest's Electras would be taken out of the air that very day. Quesada described Nyrop as being extremely distraught for completely natural reasons and said he believed Nyrop honestly did not remember how emotionally affected he was in the days following the Tell City tragedy. The author, in reconstructing the meeting, had to go along with how the majority recalled the events that transpired that day.]

It took a woman, naturally, to reduce the tension and clear the storm that had swirled around Nyrop's unbowed but unhappy head. Her name was Jean Friedkin, the blond, attractive wife of Pacific Southwest Airways president Ken Friedkin. PSA had only four planes—all Electras—at the time, but Jean Friedkin figured the tiny intrastate carrier had a voice in the proceedings.

"We're opposed to grounding," she announced.

Quesada looked at her in mingled awe and anger.

"Just who are you?" he demanded.

"I'm with PSA," she said calmly.

"Only Electra operators are supposed to be here," Quesada growled, sparing himself the luxury of a brief but burning glare in Spurgeon's direction.

"I'm vice-president of PSA," Jean Friedkin snapped with as much dignity as an outraged woman could muster. She was, too—the highest-ranking woman airline official in the country.

Quesada did something he had never done either in

wartime or in the FAA. He retreated with a hasty apology. The little exchange had not only drawn some welcome chuckles but had enabled the FAA chief to get the unruly meeting under a semblance of control.

He said it was Nyrop's privilege and right to say what he wanted to say and do what he wanted to do. But the FAA administrator added that he personally did not feel that grounding was necessary. All available evidence indicated that the additional speed restrictions provided a very adequate margin of safety while the exact cause of the two accidents was being determined. Therefore the Federal Aviation Agency would proceed along the lines he had outlined.

The meeting was adjourned. A number of airline executives surrounded Nyrop and pleaded with him not to go through with his announced intentions. This time they were friendly and warmly sympathetic instead of angry and even abusive. Nyrop, a proud, hard-hitting, and courageous aviation veteran who had kept his comparatively small airline competitive with the giants, probably would have stuck to his guns if his colleagues had continued to lash at him as they had during the meeting. But under their calmer persuasion he finally relented. Northwest would go along with the others and—although he didn't say it aloud—would pray that the FAA's program would work.

There were a lot of prayers along that line, unspoken and otherwise. One of the men who attended the dramatic session in the solarium commented later:

"I'm not one of Pete Quesada's fans and never have been. But on this particular occasion, he was magnificent. He was dignified and forceful. Grounding the Electra would have been the easiest way out for him and he would have had one hundred percent backing from Congress and the press. But he refused to panic under pressure. He would have been a hero if he had grounded the plane and stood a damned good chance of being a villain if he didn't and another one went down. That was Pete Quesada's finest hour. He just displayed sheer guts!"

That comment was not one whit exaggerated. Quesada's decision not to ground the Electra put his own career as a government official and public servant squarely on the line. More than one congressman, including Senator Hartke who said it publicly, muttered that Quesada had been a vice-president of Lockheed and that his defense of the Electra seemed to be suspect in motive.

Quesada *had* been a top Lockheed official before President Eisenhower appointed him as head of the new FAA. But he had left Lockheed because of a major disagreement on management policy. The truth was that Quesada had no love for the Burbank company and the feeling was mutual. There were plenty of sincere critics of his no-grounding decision, but nobody had any grounds for claiming that decision had been made because of his former connection with the Electra's manufacturer.

On March 25, 1960, the following telegram went out to all U.S. airlines flying the giant turboprop:

Pursuant to authority contained in the Federal Aviation Act of 1958 the following airworthiness regulation applicable to all operators of Lockheed model 188 series is effective immediately upon receipt of this telegram. Since issuance of FAA emergency regulation telegram dated March 20, 1960, it has been determined that further precautionary restrictions are necessary in the interest of safety. Therefore the emergency airworthiness regulation dated March 20, 1960, is hereby amended to read as follows: Quote: applies to all Lockheed model 188 series aircraft. Compliance required as indicated. A. Post following two placards in full view of pilot: (1) following operating speeds to be observed, $V^{ne}$ normal operating speed equal to 225 knots CAS or mach number 0.55; $V^{ne}$ never exceed speed equal to 245 knots CAS or mach number 0.55. (2) feather propeller in event the torquemeter indicator should go to zero or full scale in flight. B. The Federal Aviation Agency approved air speed limitations section of airplane flight manual is hereby amended to incorporate above speed values. C. Deactivate autopilot until FAA-approved modifications covered in Lockheed alert service bulletin number 453 are incorporated. D. Refueling procedures recommended in Lockheed service airgram FS/238716W dated 23 October 1959 shall be followed. Unquote. The rough air penetration speeds specified in the Lockheed 188 operating manual remain unchanged. This regulation will be amended as warranted. E. R. Quesada, Administrator, Federal Aviation Agency.

That was it. The die was cast not only for Lockheed, the Electra, and the airlines, but also for the one-time commander of the Ninth Air Force, who a long time ago had angered the Pentagon by taking a fellow general named Eisenhower for a ride in a single-seater fighter. Then he had been accused of risking the valuable life of a top military field leader. Now he was being accused of risking the lives of the thousands who would continue to ride an airliner that already had claimed ninety-seven victims in two crashes shrouded in mystery.

"If another one goes down," an FAA official remarked, "Pete might as well be on board."

Actually the risk was a carefully calculated one. Stripped of technical verbiage, the telegram simply meant that the FAA had considered all the then known possible causes of Tell City and Buffalo and taken precautions against their occurring again.

The key order was the restriction on speed. Literally, it brought the Electra down to the performance level of a DC-6 or Constellation. Inasmuch as the Electra wing structural tests had demonstrated a strength equal to or greater than that of those two older planes, what the restriction achieved was an additional airload margin of fifty percent.

In other words, at approximately twenty percent lower speeds, the capability of the Electra's wings to handle maximum loads in normal operations was increased fifty percent. Both the Braniff and Northwest planes had been cruising faster than a DC-6 or Constellation would under most circumstances, so even if there was some unknown, as yet undetermined wing deficiency, presumably it would not be dangerous at reduced speeds.

It never was publicized, but there had been an Electra speed restriction imposed by Lockheed voluntarily only one month after the Texas accident. Lockheed was conducting a flight test to determine what would happen if the hydraulic boost system for the controls were disconnected during the maximum allowable dive speed of four hundred and five knots.

On the second dive, turbulence was encountered and the speed slackened slightly. The pilots noticed fuel leaking from under the right wing. Ground inspection re-

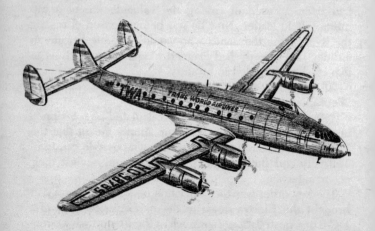

*Constellation*

vealed that some rivets had popped loose, and in addition there was a slight buckling of a rear wing beam just inside the number four nacelle.

Lockheed promptly advised Electra operators to hold down speeds until a "fix" could be made. This consisted of reinforcing the wing between the inboard and outboard nacelles, but the difficulty was not considered major. Nor was there any connection established between this incident and the Buffalo crash. The damage to the corresponding rear beams on the wings of the Braniff Electra in no way resembled that of the test flight.

The disconnecting of the autopilot stemmed from several instances of Electras "porpoising" in flight. These were traced to autopilot malfunctions, and Lockheed already had obtained FAA approval of improvements in the system that would prevent such motion. The porpoising effect did not seem severe enough to fail a wing, but no chances were being taken.

The same reasoning was behind the order for strict adherence to recommended fueling procedures. The Electra's fast-pressure fueling system on a few occasions had caused apparently minor damage to wing components when over-pressurization occurred. Lockheed had developed a "fix" involving the simple process of drilling a one-sixteenth-of-an-inch hole in a valve. It eliminated any possibility of a pressure build-up.

Aside from the order affecting Electra operations, there was FAA's directive requiring accelerated inspections on all the prop-jets being flown by U.S. carriers. This stirred up a new fuss and fresh demands for grounding.

Early in April the CAB was advised that of the first forty-one planes to be inspected, thirty-nine were found to have cracked wing-clip rivets. These small metal rectangular tabs tie the ribs and cross-members of the wings together, using four rivets on each tab.

Neither FAA nor Lockheed was particularly concerned over this revelation. There are no less than two thousand, seven hundred and fifty-four clips in an Electra. The inspectors found not more than seven sheared clips in any single airplane. And for that matter, if the inspectors had checked almost any DC-6, DC-7, Constellation, or any other airliner at random, they undoubtedly would have uncovered similar cracks in about the same proportion.

But the CAB thought the location of the cracks might indicate a developing pattern of breaks which, if allowed to go on uncorrected, conceivably could lead to serious weakening of the wing.

On April 13 the Board unanimously voted to recommend that the Electra be grounded until all ninety-six planes then flying in the United States could be inspected. The recommendation, adopted and handed to Quesada in utmost secrecy, fell far short of Slattery's more drastic proposals. He favored grounding until the two crashes were solved, and he had considerable support from some of the Bureau of Safety's engineers.

But the Board, apparently swayed by the anti-grounding arguments advanced at the meeting in the solarium three weeks before, backed away from an all-out position.

Quesada invited the five Board members to another secret meeting at his office the next day. They restated their views and Quesada quietly but firmly rejected them. It was agreed, however, that to avoid causing any public alarm, the CAB's grounding recommendation would be kept confidential. Both Quesada and the CAB were well aware what would happen if it were leaked that one federal air agency had advised grounding and the other had refused. The public, most of whom probably could not have been able to tell the difference between CAB and FAA except that they had only one initial in common, would have been understandably confused.

It leaked anyway, presumably from an unknown source within the CAB.

On April 15 Senator Hartke, who by this time was

engaged in a one-man Congressional anti-Electra crusade, phoned Quesada.

"Is it true the CAB recommended grounding?" he asked with no preliminary chitchat.

"Yes," Quesada answered with equal brevity.

"What are you going to do about it?"

"Nothing," said the FAA boss.

Hartke literally went into orbit. He summoned reporters to an impromptu news conference, revealed the grounding recommendation and Quesada's refusal, and called for a Congressional investigation.

"I am shocked," Hartke said indignantly, "that General Quesada would take the chance of ignoring the CAB's recommendation and risk further death from these planes. I hope the Senate Aviation Subcommittee will look into Quesada's failure to act in accordance with the recommendation."

Quesada was acting, but not in accordance with the recommendation. He was blowing his stack—in private, unfortunately, because it would have made interesting reading. His opinion of Hartke, in the words of an FAA aide, was that the senator seemed to regard the Northwest Electra's falling on Indiana soil as a personal affront. Publicly Quesada did not answer Hartke's blast, and it was Gross of Lockheed who issued a statement designed to offset public bewilderment at the CAB-FAA disagreement.

"Of all the wing clips examined," Gross pointed out calmly, "only five-hundredths of one percent have been found damaged. Such finds are not unusual at the traditional overhaul period of airplanes in service and there is nothing unusual in this one, either.

"We wish to assure the public and all interested parties that the findings do not affect the flight safety or the structure or the flying characteristics of the airplane. In our considered opinion, the Electra is fully safe and airworthy."

Hartke, asked about the Lockheed statement, took another swing at the FAA chief.

"If I were in General Quesada's position," he declared, "I most certainly would take the advice of the CAB."

Long after Quesada left FAA, he quietly explained to this writer some of his reasoning behind his refusal to ground the Electra—in addition to the all-important fact that he considered that the speed restrictions, inspection program, and other precautionary steps were more than sufficient protection for the public.

"I never considered the economic effects of grounding on the airlines involved," he said. "Frankly, I don't think they could have gone through it without some harmful effects. It's true they had a lot of piston-engine equipment to use in the Electra's place, but much of it was mothballed. It's possible, if I had grounded the Electra, some people might have been killed in some weary old plane pulled out of mothballs. Anyway, I didn't let myself get into the area of economics. The decision not to ground was based on technical knowledge and without emotion.

"You're damned right I was worried. I knew one more crash and I was finished. Some of the pressure for grounding came from within FAA itself—as a means of self-preservation. After all, the federal government had certificated the plane as completely safe. I didn't certificate the plane myself; that happened before FAA was created. But I never used this as an excuse even though it would have been a good out, not only for grounding but later on when we found out what was wrong with the plane.

"As for my former connection with Lockheed, I left them with ill will. I can't put it any more strongly than that. If I had been motivated by personal feelings, I would have grounded the aircraft in thirty seconds. But by my code, a public servant can never be influenced by personal feelings toward any group or individual.

"I took the attitude that the law was put in my hands to do for the public what the public could not do for itself, and no vested interest should hold the pen that writes the rule."

After the no-grounding decision. Quesada got nightly crank calls demanding that he pull the Electra out of service. One man wrote him that if the FAA and the airlines were so sure the Electra was safe, they should insure every passenger for one million dollars. And some pilots, hitherto staunch defenders of the airliner they called "the pilot's airplane," were beginning to have doubts.

Braniff and Northwest crews in particular, closer to the twin tragedies than pilots of other airlines, favored grounding. A delegation of Northwest captains called on President Nyrop and relayed the information that all Northwest ALPA councils would back grounding. Nyrop, who had given his word at the March 23 meeting, had to refuse.

Pilot sentiment was by no means unanimous on the subject, however. American and Eastern crews supported Quesada's decision. ALPA began a poll of members qualified on Electras, starting with National. The poll involved two simple, direct questions:

1. Do you favor going along with the program to fly the Electra without knowing the cause of the Braniff and Northwest accidents? [Twenty-five National pilots said yes, only three voted no.]

2. Do you want to ground the airplane until the cause of the two accidents is determined? [Twenty-five replied no, only three favored grounding.]

ALPA's director of engineering and safety, scholarly-looking Ted Linnert, and assistant Carl Eck took off on a tour covering thousands of miles and hundreds of personal interviews with Electra flight crews. They found overwhelming opposition to grounding—an amazing reaction from traditionally conservative men, and one that underlined the tremendously favorable impression the Electra had made on them.

After this trip, Linnert and Eck were about convinced continuation of a formal poll was unnecessary. They called off the poll definitely after receiving reports from no fewer than four responsible sources that the speed restrictions were adequate for safety—the National Aeronautics and Space Administration (NASA), Boeing, Douglas, and Lockheed itself, which already had called in its two chief competitors to work together toward a final solution. Linnert also had sold Lockheed on the necessity of getting information on its test and research program to pilots as quickly as possible, a move which helped solidify pilot support for the maligned plane.

ALPA's own files were beginning to get clogged with correspondence from pilots suggesting their own solutions.

"Inadvertent Beta range operation" was one pilot suspicion—the accidental reversal of a propeller in flight. Reverse pitch on a plane's props means that their angle of bite is changed, so they flatten against the wind and act as a giant brake. On the ground, that is. If a prop reversed in the air, it would be like hitting a brick wall. This had been the cause of two previous accidents involving another prop-jet airliner, the British-made Viscount. But a subsequent wiring modification made it impossible for a Viscount's props to reverse until the wheels were firmly on the ground. The same reverse-pitch lockout had been incorporated into the Electra, however, and the suggestion quickly joined the mounting pile of discarded theories.

A Western captain wrote that a possible menace involved the proximity of certain electrical units to the center wing-section tank. This already had been considered and rejected. Several pilots were worried about reports of loose bearings in the elevator balance-weight system which caused excessive vibration. But Lockheed already was aware of this and was changing over to a new bearing design.

Perhaps the most startling theory (and in retrospect the only amusing development of the Electra story) was the "blue-room crisis," as ALPA officials in Chicago dubbed it.

The "blue room" in every airliner is what crews call the lavatory. Linnert received a number of pilot letters reporting that the Electra blue room might be an area of suspicion. On infrequent occasions, always at high altitudes with extremely low temperatures, a large ice ball would accumulate on the drain through leakage. When it broke away from the aircraft, it usually would bounce off the horizontal stabilizer on the tail.

Technically speaking, an ice ball hitting the Electra's huge tail section would have about as much effect as a paper spitball. But Linnert dutifully relayed the reports to Lockheed, which corrected the situation by installing new valves and seals on the drain. Lockheed could not resist pointing out, in a subsequent service bulletin, that "proper cleaning and servicing of the lavatory plays a large part in determining whether leakage will occur."

The solution of the "blue-room crisis," however, demonstrated how everyone connected with the Electra was grasping at even the most fantastic, obscure, and remote ideas. For example, an Eastern captain reported that a cleaning compound had accidently entered a Constellation's static ports connected to flight instruments. The instrument readings were normal until the plane encountered heavy rain, at which point sizable errors were observed.

"I feel this possibility should be explored by the Electra investigating committee," he wrote.

All the various theories, wild and reasonable, farfetched and plausible, promising and impossible, were by now beginning to grind through the mills of unprecedented scientific research.

At two locations more than three thousand miles apart— NASA's mammoth wind-tunnel installation at Langley Field, Virginia, and behind the walls of Lockheed's sprawling Burbank plant—the areas of suspicion were being narrowed down to the point where the moment of truth was about to dawn.

# 5

## Achilles' Heel

Lockheed and the Civil Aeronautics Board concentrated their search for the killer of two airliners and ninety-seven human beings in two areas—the air and the laboratory.

Lockheed even gave the search an official name: Lockheed Electra Achievement Program. With the American propensity for boiling titles and names down to mere initials, it quickly became known as Operation LEAP.

The wreckage from Buffalo and Tell City was still en route to Burbank when Lockheed test pilots, sometimes with CAB and FAA technicians aboard, began some of the most hair-raising, daring experimental flights in aviation history. They not only braved destruction but actually sought it.

They crammed an Electra full of electronic instruments that followed, gauged, recorded, and measured the strain and stress from every motion of every movable part on the airplane. They pointed the ship's sleek nose in the direction of the Sierra wave—a California mountain area known for violent, almost terrifying perpetual turbulence, where updrafts were like miniature tornadoes and twisting wind shears knifed their unseen paths across the sky.

They flew with light loads, medium loads, maximum allowable loads, and loads that an Electra wasn't even designed to carry. They flew at low speeds, normal speeds, and speeds violating the "red-line" limit beyond which the plane was not supposed to be operated. The test crews worked two ten-hour shifts seven days a week, accumulating more than three million separate data items in sixty-nine separate flights. Lockheed pioneered in the field of in-flight load measurements, developing in 1949 the basic method of determining accurately wing loads in flight now used by all U.S. airplane manufacturers. The experience was a tremendous asset in these tests.

Daily the test Electra rammed her snout into the Sierra wave at speeds ranging from 200 to more than 324 knots. Once, the pilots deliberately dove the plane until the indicated air speed hit 405 knots, forty-one knots faster than the certification test dive and with a full gross load of 83,000 pounds. Then they pulled back sharply on the yoke in a vain effort to pull the wings off.

They simulated emergency collision-avoidance maneuvers. They went looking for the worst turbulence by flying low over the mountain ranges until the instruments told them where was the roughest air. Then they made repeated runs back and forth through the same turbulence at successively increasing speeds. The bouncing was so bad that an accompanying camera plane, obtaining five miles of film records, frequently could not keep the test flights in range or focus.

The sixty-nine missions represented about fifteen hundred miles of flight through moderate to extremely heavy turbulence producing gusts greater than had ever been recorded on a commercial aircraft.

Douglas, like Boeing, was ignoring completely the intense commercial rivalry existing among aircraft manufacturers, and sent over a new $80,000 device for inducing wing flutter. It consisted of vanes mounted on the wing tips. Controlled from the cockpit, they could be set at different angles, and their flapping was capable of creating frightening fluctuations even in non-turbulent air. In the Sierra wave region the Electra was shaken like a stick in the mouth of a playful dog.

Douglas had developed the vanes for use in its DC-8 jetliner test program. It offered the device because at this stage, Lockheed and the CAB were just about convinced that the Buffalo and Tell City accidents involved some kind of flutter phenomenon.

There is flutter present in every aircraft. It is caused by the turbulence of air over a plane's fast-moving surfaces. The trick is to keep it from going unchecked into an uncontrolled, continuous cycle that eventually will drive even new metal into destructive fatigue—like bending a wire back and forth until it breaks. Douglas itself had gone so far as to create abnormal flutter by exploding shotgun shells in a DC-8 wing.

The ability of an airplane to absorb and control flutter is known as damping. The Electra's precertification tests had shown the plane to have excellent flutter-damping characteristics at and above normal operating speeds. When turbulence "excited" the wing, for example, a slight lessening of speed would remove this external driving force and the flutter would dissipate. Like every airplane wing, the Electra's was designed to flex and recoil, thus absorbing energy from the oscillation. But suppose there was some external exciting force other than turbulence, a reasonable assumption inasmuch as there had been no turbulence over Buffalo?

What could have been the source of such a deadly force? The control surfaces—elevators and/or ailerons? The CAB found no indication of trouble in these components. And subsequent wind-tunnel tests demonstrated beyond question that the control surfaces, no matter what went wrong with them, never could produce wing oscillations of destructive proportions.

But the LEAP flight tests suddenly supplied a faint clue, a fleeting glimmer of something that was not quite right. From the instruments hooked to various structural innards came data revealing that the outboard nacelle structures, under extremely heavy motion loads, were taking more of a beating than anyone had thought possible.

In more specific terms, the Sierra wave tests revealed that severe and extreme turbulence put a bending force on the outer wing section from the outboard nacelles to the tips that was ten times greater than on the rest of the wing.

Now the hunt began for solid evidence of flutter not only in the wings, but in those outboard nacelles. And it did not take the metallurgists long to find it.

When the Braniff and Northwest wreckage arrived in Burbank, engineers quickly began re-examination of the former's left wing and the latter's right wing—the ones that had failed first. And special attention was given to the number one nacelle structure from Buffalo and the number four from Tell City. These were the outboard engine packages.

The Northwest wreckage provided the clearest clues. The right wing structure between the fuselage and the inboard nacelle showed numerous indications of damage progression during rapid reversals of loading. In simpler terms, the wing had been subjected to uncontrolled and massive flutter severe enough to cause failure. For example, the area at which separation from the fuselage had occurred had sustained a type of metal damage that could have resulted only from the wing's folding rearward instead of upward, as would have happened if the failure had resulted from a high up-gust or positive maneuver. Another key wing structural area displayed saw-toothed diagonal fractures which told only one thing to a metallurgist: powerful oscillation loads occurring in a repetitive cycle and consistent only with catastrophic flutter.

The number four nacelle structure, too, contained startling evidence of flutter. There were scratches of a vibrating nature found on the outside of an air inlet called the sugar scoop. The Lord mounts (named after the firm that made them, the Lord Manufacturing Company), which held the huge engine in the nacelle, had "bottomed" fifty to sixty times at a rate of 2.5 times a second for up to twenty seconds. It was further proof of violently destructive flutter.

So was the condition of the torque housing, which had been separated from the compressor case and bore marks of repeated cycles in the area of the bolt attachments. So did a vane located near the engine exhaust; it was scarred by elliptical scratches obviously reflecting violent movements of that portion of the engine casing.

Why hadn't flutter been suspected at Buffalo? The truth is that the Braniff wreckage did not show as much evidence of a continuing flutter cycle as did the Northwest plane. The left wing of the Braniff Electra, for instance, lacked many of the flutter-damage characteristics found in the right wing of the Northwest Electra. The fractures were more of a type associated with failure resulting from a high positive load, such as might occur in a sharp pull-up at high speed. It bothered many experts (and still does) that Tell City was not an exact mirror image of Buffalo.

But there still were some significant similarities, particularly in the outboard nacelles on the wings that had failed. In Northwest's number four engine and Braniff's number one, the front compressor blades had left marks on the inside of the air-inlet housing which could have come only from repeated vibration. And as in the case of the Northwest plane, the Lord mounts on the Braniff engine showed evidences of repeated rubbing and oscillation.

The mystery was far from solved, however. If flutter had attacked the two planes, how could it have been allowed to progress to the point of structural failure? Turbulence obviously was an accessory to the crime at Tell City and perhaps was the force that originally triggered flutter. But again, there had been no turbulence present at Buffalo. Furthermore, how could destructive flutter develop in a plane that had passed every known test for damping, that was known to be as flutter-free as any aircraft ever built?

Could the design of the wing itself be at fault? Could it somehow have developed an unknown weakness that escaped all the original tests? Or was the Electra's speed a factor?

Lockheed tried—and failed—to produce destructive flutter at speeds up to 550 miles per hour. It then took an entire Electra wing, complete with engines, mounted it on a rig and proceeded to destroy it with various forces ranging from powerful twists to bone-rattling shakes. By the time the hydraulic jacks supplying these forces ultimately were brought to their most vicious level, the wing already had survived torture exceeding the FAA's own requirements for strength. Yet there was confirmation of that annoying, elusive hint of trouble first disclosed by the Sierra flight tests: there was something wrong with the outboard nacelles.

The Electra recalled from Northwest's fleet, a plane with about the same logged flight hours as the Tell City aircraft, also was subjected to the so-called static tests as the wing that had been wrecked deliberately. From all the engineers could determine, the plane could have absorbed this punishment indefinitely. But once again, those outer nacelles were causing concern.

Each day Bob Gross met with all Lockheed department heads and key engineers. Each day he asked the same question:

"Do you have all the people you need and all the equipment you need? If not, we'll get it."

They took him at his word.

From the company's Georgia plant and from its missiles-and-space division came a fresh influx of technicians, scientists, engineers. Giant electronic computers were yanked unceremoniously from other projects and assigned to LEAP with a "stay with it until it's finished" order.

Flight-test data analysts went on three shifts a day,

seven days a week. Some of the engineers were working an eighty-four-hour weekly trick. And Lockheed was not ashamed to borrow talent from the outside, including personnel from rival companies. Boeing sent over a half-dozen crack aerodynamic specialists who were assigned to interpreting, checking, and analyzing the laboratory and flight-test results. This was in addition to the aid Douglas already had sent in the form of the flutter vanes. The spectacle of Lockheed's two bitterest competitors in the commercial-transport field pitching in to help was both commendable and significant. It underlined the seriousness with which the entire industry viewed the Electra's misfortunes. Where safety begins, competition ends, for public confidence is the pillar supporting all civil aviation. Any unsolved accident is a challenge to every airline and every airframe manufacturer, no matter what individual carrier or individual aircraft is involved. Buffalo and Tell City were not only unsolved crashes, but disasters that raised doubts about the industry's very system of designing and testing new planes. Lockheed's methods of developing and testing the Electra were almost identical to those used by other companies.

From the California Institute of Technology, from private electronics firms, came additional computers to sift through the mountain of accumulating data.

Lockheed also commissioned one of the nation's outstanding meteorologists.

"Find out what the weather was at Tell City," he was told. "Consult with any other weather expert you like. Fly wherever you need to. We want to know to what extent turbulence existed over Indiana that day, how wide an area it covered, how strong it was, how long it lasted."

At the Allison plant in Indianapolis, General Motors technicians dismantled all eight engines from the two accidents and subjected them to microscopic inspection. An Allison-owned Electra began flight tests of its own, concentrating on every known power-plant emergency, discrepancy, or difficulty.

"This undertaking," an official Lockheed background statement to the nation's press declared, "spreads across the entire panorama of aviation science. Investigators cannot afford to overlook any avenue. As they proceed down each, the search will become narrower. It is narrowing already."

It was.

There are more than one hundred different kinds of flutter. Modes, they are called. One hundred individual ways in which metal can vibrate. The searchers began checking out each one. And they had, by now, a pretty good idea which mode they were looking for.

The damage marks on Braniff's number one propeller displayed signs of its having wobbled. There was the sound witnesses had heard that clear September night. When the tape recording of an overspeeding prop had been played, several remarked, "That's it." An overspeeding prop on an Electra was known to present no particular menace or danger. But suppose the overspeeding was merely a symptom of something else that was wrong in the power plant?

In Indianapolis, in Burbank, in NASA's Langley wind tunnels, the investigators tried every form of flutter mode in the book and tried to link it to the overspeeding prop.

They found one. During this single mode, the propeller tips approached sonic velocity without any increase in revolutions per minute or air speed. On May 5, 1960, while more than one hundred and fifty Electras the world over plodded shamefacedly at the speeds of DC-6s and Constellations, a Lockheed engineer stood up at a meeting of CAB and FAA officials and spoke six fatal words:

"We're pretty sure it's whirl mode."

Whirl mode was nothing new. It was not a mysterious phenomenon. It was far from an unknown force. As a matter of fact, it is a form of vibrating motion inherent in any piece of rotating machinery such as oil drills, table fans, and automobile drive shafts.

As far back as the early 1930s, the application of whirl mode to the airplane propeller was a subject discussed in technical journals. Two physicists published a lengthy paper about it in 1938. Dr. Robert Scanlon, professor of aeroelasticity at the Case Institute of Technology, studied and wrote about whirl mode as recently as 1950. Scanlon and other scientists also referred to it as propeller auto-precession, propeller-nacelle whirl flutter, and gyro-flutter.

The theory was devastatingly simple and, purely hypothetically up to now, also devastating. A propeller has gyroscopic tendencies. In other words, it will stay in a smooth plane of rotation unless it is displaced by some strong external force, just as a spinning top can be made to wobble if a finger is placed firmly against it. The moment such a force is applied to a propeller, it reacts in the opposite direction.

Suppose the force drives the propeller upward. The stiffness that is part of its structure promptly resists the force and pitches the prop forward. Each succeeding upward force is met by a protesting downward motion. The battle of vibration progresses. The propeller continues to rotate in one direction, but the rapidly developing whirl mode is vibrating in the opposite direction. The result, if the mode is not checked, is a wildly wobbling gyroscope that eventually begins to transmit its violent motion to a natural outlet—the wing.

But not by the farthest stretching of the imagination was whirl mode considered dangerous to an aircraft at the time the Electra was tested and certificated. Whirl mode did develop occasionally in piston-engine planes. But it always encountered the powerful stiffness of the entire engine-nacelle structure and remained stable without spreading to the main wing area. Sooner or later, when it could not conquer that stiffness, it simply was quelled and rendered harmless. If its violence persisted, the prop finally would separate from the engine. The engine itself, therefore, was the safety valve for whirl mode. No one had dreamed that the same thing would not happen in an Electra. After all, even with turbine or jet engines it still was a propeller-driven aircraft.

What was there in the Electra's engine package that lowered the barrier to whirl mode?

Like hounds suddenly catching the scent of an elusive rabbit, the searchers went back to the nacelle structure housing the massive turbines. Again, the number four outboard of the Northwest plane. Again, the number one outboard of the Braniff plane.

In the Northwest engine a longeron, or strut fitting, failed in a clean tension break. This permitted the front end of the engine support to move upward and to the left. The Lord mounts had been subjected to abnormal loads in various directions. There were curved scratches on certain engine parts that could have come only from large cyclic motions of virtually the entire engine. The propeller reduction gearbox (which keeps the props from revolving as fast as the turbines) had been fractured, again from vicious loads in many directions.

In the Braniff engine, support struts had been bent in multiple directions. The fuel line was bent both up and down. Electrical connections had failed in multiple directions of bending. The mounts holding the reduction gearbox showed evidences of repeated motion loads.

It all meant a finding that up to now was the most important step forward in the solution of the two crashes: It was not only the propellers that had wobbled on those outboard nacelles, but the entire engine package. The next step was to learn whether a weakened nacelle structure could create whirl mode.

Lockheed built a scale model of the Electra one-eighth the size of the real airplane. It was sent to NASA's wind-tunnel facility at Langley and placed on a special mount designed by Boeing. The mount allowed the model to simulate the flight movements of an actual aircraft.

There is an NASA technical memorandum in the files of the Federal Aviation Agency. It has a blue cover, it contains eighty-three pages of tests, photographs, graphs, and charts, and it bears the imposing title of "Investigation of ⅛ Size Dynamic-Aeroelastic Model of the Lockheed Electra Airplane in the Langley Transonic Dynamics Tunnel."

The last paragraph reads in part:

"With the model configuration most nearly simulating the undamaged airplane, no dynamic-aeroelastic instabilities were encountered within the normal simulated flight range of the airplane. With simulated damage in the nacelle area, propeller autoprecession, a self-sustained, wobbling motion of the spinning propeller involving coupling of gyroscopic and aerodynamic forces, occurred."

A fifty-one-word verdict on what had gone wrong with the Electra. A fifty-one-word solution to the most mysteri-

*Scale Model*

ous, alarming crashes in aviation history. A fifty-one-word explanation of why two immensely powerful wings had snapped like matchsticks. A fifty-one-word epitaph for ninety-seven innocent victims of aviation's rare but deadly imperfections and assumptions.

The Electra's Achilles' heel was in those outboard engine nacelles. What NASA scientists had done was to weaken the struts and braces that held the engine firmly in the nacelle package. They "flew" the model at speeds equal to and exceeding those of the Braniff and Northwest planes. Then at those speeds they created a sudden jolt that excited the weakened nacelle. Whirl mode started, spread, and devoured the wing itself.

Basically the trouble had nothing to do with the Electra's strength. It involved stiffness—stiffness of the nacelle structure. Stiffness is not the same as strength. If one confuses the two, it is like thinking glass and air are the same because both are transparent. And in an airplane, stiffness is the chief resistant force against flutter. What had happened to the Electra was devastating in its deadly simplicity.

First there had to be prior damage in the outboard nacelles, some weakening of the braces and struts. It never has been determined definitely what nacelle damage was inflicted on either the Buffalo or Tell City plane prior to its last flight. The alleged hard landing the Northwest plane made at Chicago might have been a source. There was absolutely no indication of what could have resulted in prior nacelle damage to the Braniff Electra.

But whatever the birth of such damage, there was no doubt of what it could lead to. It reduced the nacelle's stiffness to the point where a sudden jolt at high speed from turbulence or a sharp upward maneuver resulted in the engine wobbling in its mount.

The Electra's turbines spin at thirteen thousand, eight hundred and twenty revolutions per minute. The propellers turn at twelve hundred and eighty RPMs. The entire package is nothing but a big gyroscope. And a jolt was a giant finger reaching out and touching this smoothly whirring mass, causing it to break stride and wobble.

As the agitated engine began to wobble, so did the propeller, with its normal plane of rotation disturbed. As the prop wobbled, its violently uneven motion was transmitted to the wing. The wing, too, began to flex and flutter. This in turn sent additional discordant forces back to the engine-prop package, which began wobbling even more wildly. By now, whirl mode was well into its unending cycles, each feeding the mode new energy.

The next step in this chain reaction was the tendency of uncontrolled whirl mode to slow down in frequency even as it increased in violence. That frequency would be about five cycles per second at the start. But unchecked, whirl mode reduced in frequency to three cycles per second. That happened to be the same maximum frequency at which the Electra wing could flutter. The moment the two vibration frequencies touched the same level, the effect was comparable to a sustained high note's eventually breaking a glass tuned to the same vibration level. Harmonic or dynamic coupling, it is called. The estimated elapsed time between the jolt that excited the nacelle, causing whirl mode to start, and the separation of the wing was only about thirty seconds.

NASA's determination that the nacelle structure had to be damaged *before* whirl mode could become destructive was a puzzler as far as the Buffalo accident was concerned. The Braniff Electra was virtually a brand-new airplane, with no record of any hard landings, no particularly bad turbulence encountered, no incidents of violent maneuvers that might have weakened an outboard nacelle.

Also puzzling was the difference in the type of damage to the wings that failed. On the Braniff plane, failure resulted from "high positive loads"—in other words, apparently from a sharp pull-up. The wing had folded upward. On the Northwest Electra, separation followed severe flutter, and the wing had folded to the rear.

The CAB's final report on the Buffalo accident, issued nineteen months later, offered what appears to be a logical if unprovable explanation of the discrepancies.

The Board recalled that witnesses had heard the sound of a supersonic propeller about thirty seconds before the ball of fire was seen at fifteen thousand feet. NASA's experiments showed that whirl mode, from inception to destruction, takes between twenty and forty seconds, and the sound of an overspeeding, wobbling prop definitely can be associated with whirl mode.

The first impulse of a pilot, the CAB reasoned, when confronted with either severe vibration, a runaway propeller noise, or both, would be to slow the ship down. His normal and natural reaction, then, would be reduction of power and/or an immediate climb. In an Electra, which takes several minutes to reduce speed from two hundred and seventy-five knots to two hundred, climbing would be the most immediately effective method of cutting air speed.

That raises the possibility, the CAB theorized, that Captain Stone, startled by the unaccustomed noise of a runaway propeller, may have pulled back on the control yoke with such sudden pressure that he amputated a wing already weakened by whirl mode. The CAB report emphasized that this did *not* imply pilot error—i.e., that Stone applied a yoke force capable of failing a structurally sound wing—but an abrupt, sharp back pressure on the controls could have been the final blow to a wing which even then was in the process of shaking itself to death.

What diluted the stiffness of Braniff's number one nacelle structure probably will never be known. Perhaps a hard landing that was not reported. Perhaps previous turbulence that had had a greater damaging effect on the outboard nacelles than any pilot would have had a right to expect in a brand-new airplane. Perhaps the metallic cancer got its start just one week before the disaster over Buffalo, when the same Electra was used on a routine training flight.

On that flight, recovery from a planned, deliberate stall was made incorrectly and another stall developed. This was accompanied by buffeting more severe than normally experienced, but the training captain did not think it was bad enough to endanger structural integrity and he did not request an inspection. He probably was right, and even if he was wrong, no blame can possibly be attached. At this point in the Electra's life, the weakened-nacelle and whirl-mode combination was just a gleam in the Devil's eye.

# 6

# The Fix

There never really was any single dramatic moment when the great light dawned and the Electra mystery was solved. Rather it was a gradual, patient, painstaking process of elimination. The systematic, orderly breakdown of the various phenomena theoretically capable of destroying an airplane in flight. The scientific determination of the Electra's flaw—whether it was strength, whether it was flutter, whether it was aeroelasticity (the balance between a structure's stiffness and the forces that act on it), or a combination of some or all of these three factors.

Lockheed, the CAB, and FAA freely admit that if Tell City had not happened, the Buffalo accident would not have been solved for years and might never have been solved. But after Tell City, it was clear the pattern was the same. This one fact narrowed down enormously the engineering area in which the truth lay hidden. This was the area known as structural dynamics, and all other areas were eliminated before the crater in an Indiana soybean field stopped smoking.

The laboratory, wind-tunnel, and flight tests, which had strained theories, data suppositions, hypotheses, and experimentation through a scientific sieve at a cost of two and a half million dollars, finally produced the whirl mode deduction after about eight weeks of effort on the part of more than three hundred and fifty top aeronautical engineers and metallurgists.

On May 12, 1960, Bob Gross called in representatives of every airline operating Electras and gave them the verdict of those three hundred and fifty brains: unstable whirl mode.

Lockheed, after taking a deep corporate breath, also broke the news that it would foot the entire bill for modifying every Electra flying or still on the assembly line. The airlines would have to pay ferry costs of getting the planes to Burbank and then back to line duty. There were wide reports, particularly in the financial press, that the modification program cost would exceed seventy million dollars. Lockheed's own estimate on that May 12 was twenty-five million, a figure which turned out to hit actual expenditures just about on the nose.

The twenty-five million was expensive enough and inevitable. The Electra's malignancy was serious and the surgery necessarily drastic in terms of both money and scope. There had to be more computations, tests, and experiments aimed at determining exactly what could be done to the outboard nacelles for positive elimination of the whirl-mode chain reaction. Between May 5, when Lockheed announced the solution to the CAB and FAA, and May 12, when the company informed the airlines, engineers working around the clock arrived at the cure. It was, indeed, major surgery.

At the top and bottom of the reduction gearbox were installed two additional "vibration isolators"—big metal struts. The top one protected against fore and aft stresses, the bottom protected against the same stresses and also held the fort against vertical and lateral loads. The original Electra design had only side struts, one on each side.

A welded V-shaped tubular frame was attached internally to both sides of the QEC structure (the so-called Quick Engine Change panels on the outside of the nacelles). This was to assist the top skin in its structural

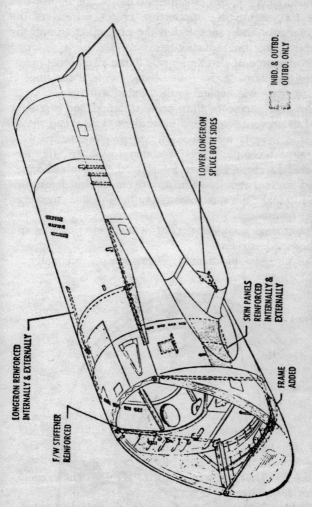

LONGERON REINFORCED
INTERNALLY & EXTERNALLY

F/W STIFFENER
REINFORCED

FRAME
ADDED

SKIN PANELS
REINFORCED INTERNALLY &
EXTERNALLY

LOWER LONGERON
SPLICE BOTH SIDES

INBD. & OUTBD.

OUTBD. ONLY

*Project LEAP Nacelle Modifications*

support. In effect, this plus the two new vibration isolators gave the engine five supporting braces instead of the original two, and concentrated the protection around the critical area of the reduction gearbox.

Reinforcements also were made to the attachment points where the "horse collar"—an oblong frame at the front of the nacelle—was hooked to the engine structure.

The rear-engine mounts were stiffened and strengthened to prevent any lateral movement. LEAP had shown that the mounts were too soft, causing premature wear and almost complete loss of ability to isolate vibration. Lockheed's stress analysis determined that only the outboard engines required this improvement, but it was decided to make the same changes in the inboard engines as bonus insurance.

Upper engine panels were stiffened, side paneling and latches made stronger.

The air inlet nicknamed "sugar scoop," originally at-

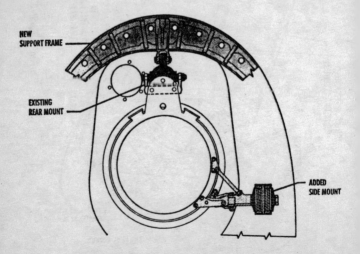

NEW SUPPORT FRAME

EXISTING REAR MOUNT

ADDED SIDE MOUNT

*Project LEAP Engine Installation Modifications*

tached to a movable engine part, was relocated because LEAP tests demonstrated that malfunction of an adjoining component was not as serious as with the sugar scoop attached. Even the shape of one nacelle part was changed because its original configuration was more prone to motion during whirl mode.

These modifications all concentrated on plugging the loophole through which disaster had poured in the skies over Buffalo and Tell City. They had the effect of almost doubling the stiffness of the nacelles.

One test in particular underlined the effectiveness of the nacelle changes. It had been determined that the worst condition, during whirl mode, was failure of the gear-reduction box housing. Such failure diminished nacelle stiffness to only seventeen percent of normal. The same test was made on a LEAP-modified nacelle with the housing intentionally fractured in advance. Even with this mass flopping around like a spaniel's ears, nacelle stiffness

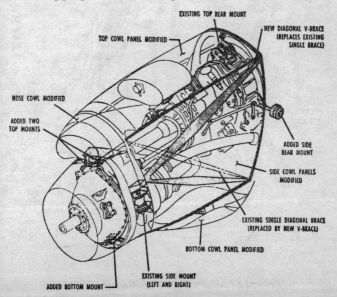

*Project LEAP Rear Engine Mount*

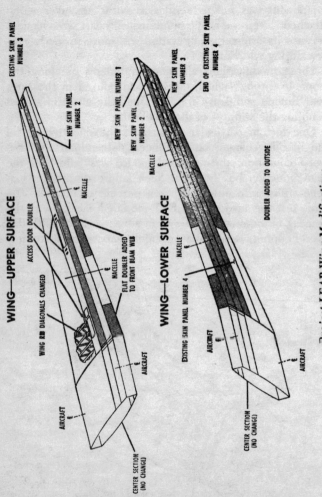

*Project LEAP Wing Modifications*

remained within ninety-six percent of a totally undamaged nacelle.

Lockheed went several steps further, however. Well aware that public and even airline confidence in the Electra had been shaken badly, LEAP's engineers decided also to embark on structural rework involving the wings, particularly the areas which LEAP had tagged as displaying merely adequate margins of structural integrity. Lockheed was determined that the new Electra would be more than just adequate.

A forward top wing plank was replaced with much heavier material. Ditto three forward bottom planks.

Double braces were added to key internal wing structural sections. Eighteen vital wing ribs were relocated to boost their resistance to twisting stresses, and these also were refabricated with heavier aluminum.

The computers clicked and whirled, the engineering graph pens scrawled their mathematically precise paths, and the results supplied powerful reassurance for anyone who would ride the Electra in the future at any speed. The wing revisions had resulted in a seven percent increase in strength and twenty percent more stiffness.

All told, the nacelle-wing modifications added no less than fourteen hundred pounds of metal to the Electra's structure.

Now Lockheed had to prove to the FAA, CAB, and its customers that the changes not only cured the disease but provided everlasting, positive immunity. So the torture racks were started up again.

A modified Electra was shaken by hydraulic jacks until engineers winced visibly from the terrible punishment. Complete nacelle packages with the stiffening improvements incorporated went through the same ordeal. Part after part was intentionally weakened, loosened, or broken beforehand to see if the worst vibration could spread the damage to the rest of the structure. This phase of testing was Lockheed's tacit admission that the "fail-safe" concept

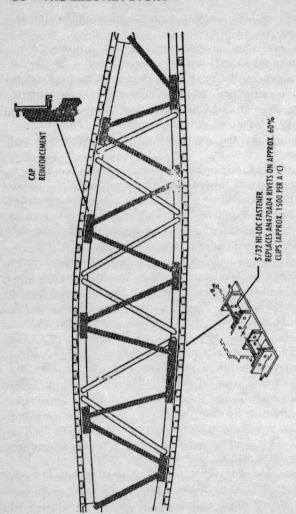

CAP
REINFORCEMENT

5/32 HI-LOC FASTENER.
REPLACES AN470AD4 RIVETS ON APPROX. 60%
CLIPS (APPROX. 1500 PER A/C)

*Project LEAP Rib Diagonals Modification*

of which it was so proud had not been extended to the area that had proved the Electra's undoing—flutter. Now that concept was being applied in earnest, providing the fattest margin of safety ever put into a commercial transport.

Late in June, Lockheed pilots began a new phase of test flights which amounted to premeditated inviting of mid-air destruction. They took four modified, company-owned Electras and once more went looking for trouble.

Was the new nacelle really stiff enough? Before each "LEAPed" Electra was allowed to take off, it sat on the end of the runway with all four engines gunned up to maximum take-off power nine times. This was to subject the nacelles to the greatest possible torque during engine acceleration.

Take-off was made at maximum climb speed, followed by a sharp climbing turn that stood the aircraft almost on its wing—again to put the worst possible strain on the entire nacelle structure. The plane was kept in this steep turn until it had clawed its way to nine thousand feet. At nine thousand a sudden power reduction, followed by a steep dive, then pull-up, landing, and the final touch—a full reverse stop in which the propellers and engines alone brought eighty-three thousand pounds of metal to a rubber-burning halt.

Exactly three thousand and twenty-nine times this before take-off full-power application was made. Satan himself could not have dreamed up a more fiendish way to test propellers, engines, gearboxes, QEC panels, and nacelles; a surer method of weakening their over-all stiffness. Only nothing weakened.

After every flight, every component in the whole engine package was subjected not only to visual but X-ray inspection. Not a brace had worked loose. Not a rivet had popped.

Again the test Electras snarled their hell-bent way toward the Sierra wave and its insidious, malevolent, unseen demons of destruction. For a total of one hundred hours they bounced and shook and rolled through turbulence, until metal groaned in anguished protest. They dove at speeds up to four hundred and thirty miles an hour with a full gross load, slammed back on the yoke, and waited in vain for gravity to tear off the wings at the roots.

They once more attached the Douglas aerodynamic vanes, or "drivers," to the wing tips, deflected them at various angles, and generated numerous flutter-causing frequencies. The wings flexed their metal muscles, but there was no chain reaction of whirl mode.

On one occasion a camera crew inside an Electra photographed a test flight involving not only these attempts to induce uncontrolled, undamped flutter, but also an outboard propeller that had been loosened so it would wobble.

A few days later, the slow-motion color film was shown to some top Lockheed executives and engineers. They watched in absolute silence as the prop went into its wild gyrations and sent its disturbed pulsations into the wing. The latter moved up and down as if it were made of rubber.

"My God," someone said in the darkened, silent room.

The wing movements became noticeably less as the damping effect took over, partly from the wing but also from the heavily stiffened nacelle. Whirl mode had been choked to death before it had scarcely begun to breathe.

The tests, both on the ground and in the air, went on for six months. The Electra passed a major FAA recertification hurdle one day when the engineers removed the reduction gearbox, complete with housing and shaft, from an outboard engine. This simulated an in-flight failure of the unit and sent the turbine's enormous torque forces spinning unchecked. The plane then was dived at speeds up to four hundred and eighteen miles per hour in this weakened condition—but again whirl mode was swallowed quickly.

On December 13, 1960, chief LEAP engineer Jack Real

flew to Washington for a conference with Oscar Bakke, FAA's Director of Flight Standards.

"We're satisfied," Real said, "but we want to know if there's anything more Lockheed can do to prove we've licked the problem."

"There is," replied Bakke. "Have you got guts enough to weaken the engine mounts deliberately, take a modified Electra beyond the never-exceed speed into extreme turbulence, and see if the wings and the new nacelle supports will dampen whirl mode?"

Real gulped. What Bakke was asking was the deliberate re-enactment of Tell City, with an actual airplane and some live guinea pigs. But he hesitated only a second.

"I said we're sure and we are," he answered quietly.

Just before Christmas, Real called in Lockheed's dozen or so test pilots and told them what the FAA wanted.

"I don't think we'll have any trouble," he added with a wry smile, "but just the same I'll ask for volunteers."

Every pilot raised his hand.

The next day engineers went to work on a LEAP Electra, which happened to be plane 1103, an aircraft just purchased by FAA itself for training and personnel transport use. They went beyond the FAA's "show us it's safe" edict, however. They removed the two original side struts not only from one outboard engine, but the other outboard and both inboards as well. Then they took out the reduction gear or torque shaft on the number four outboard to simulate a broken engine. To make the prop windmill uncontrolled with no engine power, they disconnected the pitch lock.

At this very moment they had come as close as possible to the conditions that must have existed at 3:25 P.M. March 17, 1960, except for the added factor of clear-air turbulence. The latter was supplied easily. The two test pilots chosen for the mission, "Fish" Salmon and Roy Wimmer, took off for the Sierra wave.

Although Salmon and Wimmer insisted it was not necessary, the cockpit emergency-evacuation door was rigged with a special switch for instant opening in case a wing failed. The Electra was taken up to twenty thousand feet, but was not pressurized, so the escape door could be opened in a split second. The two pilots wore oxygen masks—and also parachutes. An indestructible tape recorder was hooked to their mikes, just in case.

Salmon, a trim, handsome man with a tiny mustache that gives him the appearance of an unreformed pirate, insisted later that neither he nor Wimmer was worried.

"We were one hundred percent certain the fix was sound and we were sure nothing would happen," he recalled.

But if they weren't worried, others were.

The usual drivers, or vanes, were on the wing tips, ready to excite flutter.

Number 1103 roared toward her rendezvous. She began to buck as she penetrated turbulence.

180 knots. The vanes were tilted. No abnormal flutter.

200 knots. Still no unusual flutter.

220 knots. 240. 260. 280. Past the speed of Buffalo. 300. 320. Past the speed of Tell City. 340. 360. Beyond the never-exceed red line.

The windmilling prop was vibrating. Outboard nacelles trembled. Both wings moved up and down, up and down, in an ominous cycle. Whirl mode was under way. A faint buzz, a slight shudder—the only audible and physical manifestations of the death mode.

Vanes now were tilted to an angle designed to excite maximum flutter. If whirl mode ever was going to spread, now was the time. Once the deliberately weakened nacelles gave way, their vibration frequencies would instantly couple with those of the wings. Tell City again. Disintegration.

Salmon and Wimmer looked out at the wings. Flexing and moving, but no runaway flutter. The nacelles were pitching, but holding firm. Even without those side struts.

The fourteen hundred pounds of strategically placed, ingeniously designed reinforcements were doing the job for which they were intended. A two-and-a-half-million-dollar research prayer was being answered. The stiffer and stronger wings, the additional supports within the nacelles were damping out flutter before it could spread and couple.

Number 1103 went into a high-speed dive. 240 knots. 300 knots. Indicated air speed 346 knots. Back on the yoke. Buffalo, Texas, at 11:08 P.M. September 29, 1959.

Wings bent as the G forces clamped their stranglehold. Nacelles pitched upward. But no menacing flutter.

Number 1103 headed for her Burbank barn.

Six more times, test pilots, accompanied by FAA inspectors, exposed modified Electras to these catastrophe-loaded conditions. Six more times they failed to induce nacelle flutter that would couple in frequency to wing flutter.

On January 5, 1961, the Federal Aviation Agency announced approval of the Lockheed Aircraft Corporation's Electra modification program and removed the speed restrictions, effective immediately, from every aircraft so modified.

# 7

# Black Eye

It is a tribute to the common sense, judgment, and faith of airline passengers that they do not panic like frightened children after a bad crash. Since flying became an accepted way to travel, accidents usually have had little effect on load factors, the airlines' economic thermometer. (Load factor is the percentage of seats occupied out of the total of seats available; a hundred-passenger plane carrying seventy paying customers has a load factor of seventy percent.)

Likewise, passengers traditionally have not shied away from particular types of planes that have been involved in serious crashes. One reason is that many people pay more attention to schedule convenience and speed than to the kind of airliner on which they are traveling. The second reason is the flying public's rather surprising tendency not to indict a mere machine for a specific tragedy.

No U.S. airliner ever built has been immune from accidents, including those caused by some weakness or defect in the plane itself. That statement applies to every commercial transport from the beloved DC-3 to the modern jets introduced in the late fifties and early sixties. Yet passengers have not canceled reservations in Constellations after a "Connie" crash. They have not refused to fly in a DC-6 because a DC-6 had just gone down. There was no rush away from the Viscount in 1960 after one lost a wing over Chase, Maryland, in a thunderstorm. Even temporarily mysterious, unsolved accidents seem to bother the professionals more than the laymen. The then unexplained crash of a Boeing 707 shortly after taking off from New York's Idlewild Airport on March 1, 1962, had no effect on 707 load factors. Neither did the rash of landing-gear difficulties encountered by Boeings in 1960, nor a spate of hydraulic failures suffered by DC-8s in the summer of 1961. As a matter of fact, passenger reaction in the latter incidents significantly was far calmer than some Congressional reaction, which in certain cases approached the hysterical.

There is danger, of course, in overgeneralizing this almost tolerant public view of air accidents. Some of it undoubtedly is due to the average American's lack of technical knowledge about aircraft. Some of it stems from a faith that whatever has caused or contributed to a crash will be corrected quickly. Some of it may be just an "it

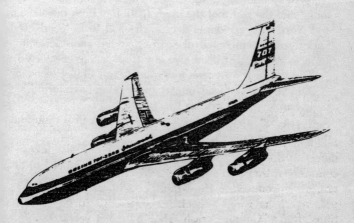

*Boeing 707*

can't happen to me" philosophy—which also happens to be the chief reason why slaughter on the highway has little deterrent effect. And finally, it is inaccurate to say that crashes do not create fear. While they do not scare most of those who fly, they unquestionably keep those who don't fly from setting foot in an airplane.

Yet it is remarkable that accidents, with two exceptions, resulted in no more than an imperceptible and very temporary drop in air travel. The first exception occurred in the 1946–48 period, when the airlines suffered noticeable drops in load factors, unusually sharp declines attributed directly to several fatal crashes in the United States alone. The load factors remained depressed for a considerable time, until public confidence was restored gradually.

But the second exception was the Lockheed Electra after Tell City, and for the first time in commercial-aviation history a crash generated fear and prejudice toward an individual airliner.

Mystery nourished additional fears, rumors fed on rumors, and the fact that the investigation of both the Braniff and Northwest accidents necessarily had to be conducted under some semblance of secrecy added more discoloration to the biggest black eye any transport ever sported.

"Did you hear American was going to sell all its Electras?"

"Did you know that Douglas and Boeing have forbidden their employees to ride in Electras?"

"It's a fact that Lockheed paid Quesada fifty thousand dollars not to ground the Electra."

Whispers. Unfounded reports. Even cruel, sick jokes.

There was a disc jockey in Miami who announced to his audience one morning, "Did you hear about the guy who said to the ticket agent, 'I'd like a ticket on the next Electra flight to New York.' And the agent replied, 'We don't sell Electra tickets, we sell chances.' "

Electra "jokes" flew around the nation faster than the plane itself. Like "Have you joined the Electra Crash of the Month yet?" Or "Don't miss that new aviation play—

*Mourning Becomes the Electra!*" Or "Have you read the new Electra book, *Look Ma, No Wings?*"

The Electra's fallen reputation even affected, of all things, the model airplane industry. Revell, Inc., world's largest manufacturer of plastic kits, had put out a replica of the turbo-prop with American Airlines insignia. Shortly after Tell City, sales of the model at airports dipped sharply, followed by similar declines at hobby stores. About a year later, when the Electra was back in the public's good graces, Revell's sales suddenly began to rise.

In the fall of 1960, FAA administrator Quesada obtained a new American League baseball franchise for Washington after the old Senators were transferred to Minneapolis. His retirement from government service was inevitable after the Democratic victory at the polls. Promptly a gag was born and circulated widely that Quesada would call the new team the "Electras"—an undisguised crack at his defense of the plane.

The rumors, the jokes, and for that matter the memory of two terrible, mystery-shrouded crashes had their devastating effects.

Even stewardesses were affected. Several airlines began to experience resistance from girls who refused to bid Electra trips—and some who did were openly reluctant about the whole thing. Not to passengers, of course, but to colleagues in the airline, to whom they admitted fear and misgivings.

How many companies actually ordered key employees and officials not to fly the prop-jet will never be known. No firm ever would admit publicly that such orders were issued. But one Civil Aeronautics Board official says that as late as the spring of 1962, about a dozen large corporations still had an Electra ban in effect. One of them was an aircraft manufacturer (not Douglas, Boeing, Convair, or Fairchild, it should be added, all of whom build transports and knew full well what had happened to Lockheed could have happened to them).

Nor will it ever be known how many passengers canceled Electra reservations or merely refused to obtain
space on one. This writer personally witnessed one incident which must have been repeated many times in the
post-Tell City period. He was sitting in a TWA lounge at
Washington National Airport when a middle-aged man
asked the receptionist to get him space on an Eastern
flight to New York. She complied. The man turned to
leave, but suddenly frowned.

"What kind of plane?" he wanted to know.

The receptionist called Eastern again.

"It's an Electra," she said.

"Get me another flight," he demanded.

To her everlasting credit, the TWA employee ignored
the fact that Eastern was a competitor and that TWA did
not operate Electras.

"Sir," she informed him bluntly, "you're being silly.
The federal government says that plane is safe, and I'm
quite sure Eastern wouldn't be flying it if it wasn't."

"I don't give a damn," the passenger snapped. "I won't
set foot in one of those things."

Reluctantly the receptionist got him space on a Constellation. After he left, the receptionist remarked to this
writer, "That's been happening almost every day."

It was, too. Every U.S. airline operating Electras admitted later that for the rest of 1960 and well into 1961, the
prop-jet's load factors declined to an alarming extent. American alone reported that in this period its Electras were
carrying up to ten percent fewer passengers than normally. American probably suffered less than the other
Electra operators, principally because it waged an aggres-
sive advertising campaign in the plane's behalf. Yet even a
ten percent drop in load factors can be economically
damaging.

Northwest's dipped from an average of more than seventy percent, before Tell City, to fifty-six percent. National's fell to forty-nine percent. Western's slumped from

seventy-seven percent to below fifty. These were just examples of a black eye becoming a mass of red ink. The only carrier whose Electra load factors stayed up was tiny Pacific Southwest.

Lou Davis, a veteran aviation writer, about this time was preparing a story for *Flying* magazine on a local service airline. Davis, in the course of interviewing ten passengers on one of the "feeder line" flights, happened to ask why they were taking this particular plane. Eight of them said they did not want to ride a faster Electra heading for the same destination as their old DC-3.

Curious, Davis made the point of questioning scores of passengers in the terminal when he arrived. He found general fear about the Electra expressed by veteran air travelers, mostly businessmen who were well versed, comparatively speaking, on aviation matters. Conversely, those first-time or seldom-fly passengers were unconcerned about the type of plane they flew. They probably would not have

known an Electra from a B-17. Davis's informal survey was stark evidence that the anti-Electra prejudice was festering where it could do the most damage—among those who supplied the airlines with the bulk of their traffic.

Some carriers went so far as to remove the very name "Electra" from their advertisements. Braniff, for example, started referring to the plane as the "L-188." Eastern began putting emphasis on its "Golden Falcon service" without referring to the aircraft itself. Some of the others merely plugged "prop-jet" service and avoided even mentioning the word Electra.

The nation's press treated the Electra's troubles objectively and without rancor. But there was one glaring exception, an editorial in the *Territorial Enterprise* of Virginia City, Nevada. The *Enterprise* did not exactly have the circulation of the *Chicago Tribune* or the prestige of the *New York Times,* but it happened to have an editor of some fame and influence, the well-known train fancier, Lucius Beebe.

Mr. Beebe, whatever his writing ability and his admirable love of the iron horse, was not known to have acquired any degree in aeronautical engineering. This did not prevent him from referring learnedly to the Electra as the "flying incinerator."

"For years it was practically impossible to pick up a newspaper but one of these incredible crates had exploded, disintegrated, caught fire or simply fallen apart while doing 300 or 400 miles per hour," Mr. Beebe wrote with gleeful venom. He labeled the plane a "well-certified death trap" and added the observation that "to fly Lockheed was a recognized and calculated form of suicide."

Lockheed's legal department promptly branded the editorial as openly libelous. But the company decided not to take action, on the theory that a libel suit merely would spread Beebe's quotes beyond the limited circulation of his rather colorful newspaper. Besides, Lockheed and its Electra customers were having enough troubles.

The speed restrictions themselves were hurting load factors. Why fly a "jinxed" airplane when you could make the same trip in almost the same time on a DC-6, DC-7, or Viscount? American's Electra schedule between Chicago and New York increased as much as eighteen minutes, ostensibly a minor change, but a major one considering that speed traditionally has been a key factor in passenger choices. Furthermore, the longer flight times and attendant rescheduling problems boosted American's direct Electra operating costs by a whopping $350,000 a month—a jump of twenty-five percent in an industry that frequently measures profits by the pennies.

Electra operators could understand and even sympathize with the fears expressed by many business firms issuing secret "don't fly the Electra" orders. But they were bitter toward companies in the aviation industry which joined privately in the chorus. Commented Bill Littlewood, American's vice-president for equipment research, with characteristic bluntness:

"We could understand it coming from people who didn't know anything about aviation, but some of these firms were in the aviation field and their attitude was ridiculous."

The dark cloud of suspicion that had fallen on the once proud Electra, the persistent rumors, some of which were coming from within the aviation industry itself, prompted one airplane manufacturer to strike back. This was Tom Harris, head of Aero Design and Engineering Company, which makes the popular Aero Commander—the first small executive aircraft to be assigned to the White House for presidential (Eisenhower's) use. Late in the fall of 1960 Harris addressed the following memorandum to all Aero Commander management personnel, a message that bears repeating in part because it was written at the low tide of the Electra's reputation and the high tide of the whispering campaign against the plane:

"I recently returned from New York on an airline Electra flight. While back East I had discussed with some people

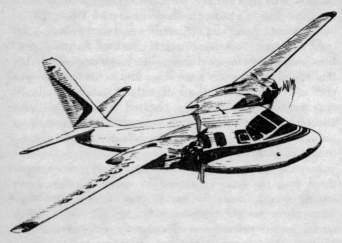

*Aero Commander*

at American Airlines the problem they had been experiencing because of public reaction to the series of Electra accidents. . . .

"In this country, the public is the final judge of what ventures or products succeed or fail. In presenting any product to the public which involves risks or dangers to the customer if that product should be improperly manufactured, the public relies principally on the reputation of those who have made and presented the product. In addition, in aviation, drugs, and many other fields, legislation or regulations also exist, promulgated by governmental bodies or agencies which must also certify the product before it can be marketed. In our own industry this is, of course, the Type Certificate issued by the FAA, certifying the airworthiness of aircraft.

"Of these two, by far greater in significance and value is, of course, the reputation of the manufacturer who acts, not only because of his responsibility to the public, but because of a matter of sound business practices as well. As manufacturers of aircraft, we know that no coercion needs to be exerted in order to make us build safe airplanes. We, as a manufacturer, are more interested in seeing to it that our product is built properly and safely than anyone else, including the federal regulatory agencies.

"When we have completed an aircraft, and are satisfied that we have produced a safe and airworthy vehicle, we must of course secure this government certification. These two things accomplished, we go to the public and do our best to persuade potential customers that this is the machine they should buy. How well we succeed depends on how effective our persuasive efforts are. We ask for no help from others. We do expect, however, that to the extent our reputation has substance, and to the extent that this government certification is valid, others in the industry will respect our claim for airworthiness. We ask no praise from competitors, but in fairness and in behalf of total industry growth, we believe under this circumstance other members of the industry should not attack, criticize or infer any unsafe situation with regard to such a product. . . .

"It [has] developed that some of our own people have opinions that the airplane is not safe to ride as presently being operated by the airlines; that it has an inherent defect which has not been determined or remedied, and that to fly in it is foolish and unwise.

"At this point, I should like to make it very clear that I do not intend to ask anyone in this organization to fly in any aircraft which he or she does not wish to fly in, either because of the opinions as to safety, comfort, or any other reason. The people of Aero Commander are free to exercise their own judgment and conscience in determining what aircraft, if any, they are individually willing to travel in.

"Having made this clear, I feel impelled also to make clear that in my opinion, as responsible members of the aircraft industry, we also have the obligation to avoid making any remarks about another manufacturer's aircraft that tend to destroy confidence in it, or impute any dangerous condition to such aircraft that would damage its reputation as well as the reputation of this industry, of which we are a part. No one is expected to make statements in praise of an aircraft that they honestly do not feel warrants praise, but an aircraft which has the reputation and experience of a sound manufacturer and the certification of the FAA should be talked about by others in our industry as being safe and airworthy, and if it cannot be praised by an individual, certainly it should not be run down.

"If we cannot say something good about airplanes such as this, I suggest that we should at least remain silent."

At this stage of the Electra's history, the word "jinx" was the most applicable description. Even its name became part of the unhappy legend being woven around the plane. A national news magazine, in an otherwise fair accounting of the prop-jet's tribulations, recalled that Electra was one of the most tragic figures in Greek mythology.

She was the daughter of King Agamemnon, who was murdered by his wife. Electra saved her brother, Orestes, from a similar fate by spiriting him away to an uncle. Throughout the years, she kept urging him to avenge their father's death. Orestes finally returned, killed his mother and her lover, and then was driven from Greece by angry gods. Some Greek tragedies depict Electra as eventually going mad from her desire for revenge and her brother's own fate.

Those who noted that the plane had tragic historical antecedents might also have remembered that in Greek, Electra means brilliant. And the aircraft was named after a star, not a mythological woman (who by some accounts was more of a heroine than a figure of murder, revenge, and tragedy).

It may seem ridiculous to comment on this admittedly

obscure connection between a character from ancient history and a twentieth-century airliner. But the article was read by millions and contributed to the "jinx" appellation that had been hung on the Electra's neck like an albatross.

There was a logical reason for the article's very appearance, however. It was written as a climax to two more Electra crashes.

On September 14, 1960, an American Electra making a routine approach at La Guardia hit a dike at the edge of the runway and flipped over. There were no fatalities, and not a few pilots commented that such an impact force would have crumpled a less sturdily built plane.

The captain, a veteran American supervisory pilot, insisted he had encountered a downdraft just before passing over the dike. The CAB said later he simply had goofed up his approach and came in too low and too short. Inasmuch as downdrafts leave behind no residual evidence of previous existence, the embittered captain was tagged with a pilot-error stigma. But La Guardia itself, a frequent breeding ground for pilot error, also was tagged as an accessory—for not having warning lights on the dike. In addition, the runway involved was considerably shorter than normal because of construction, a factor which may have caused the pilot subconsciously to try to compensate for the abbreviated length.

As in the case of the first Electra crash at La Guardia, this was an accident that could have happened to any plane. Had it not been for the Electra's past history, the prop-jet probably would have come out of the second La Guardia accident with a somewhat enhanced reputation. After all, the fuselage stayed remarkably intact, nobody had been killed, and it was noted by one rescuer that he had trouble getting the crew out of the cockpit; he couldn't break a flight deck side window even by using a heavy ax.

But still, the airliner involved was an Electra, and the word "jinx" was muttered ominously throughout the industry. On October 4 it did more than mutter. It boomed.

Shortly after 5 P.M. a fifth Electra went down, and this time there were fifty-nine fresh fatalities to further blacken the ship's name.

It was an Eastern Electra, Flight 375 from Boston's Logan International Airport to New York and points south. There were seventy-two aboard. Exactly forty-seven and one-half seconds after the pilot laconically told the tower "375 rolling," the plane was under the waters of Boston Harbor, and only ten persons survived. Both pilots and the flight engineer were among the victims and there was no immediate explanation of a most illogical crash.

The Electra had taken off normally. Just as it left the ground, it seemed to falter and yaw. It continued to climb, but only for a few seconds. Then the left wing dropped. The plane fell off into a half roll and dived into the Bay.

Engine failure on take-off was the first theory, but it was not a theory that made much sense. The Electra's reserve power was the greatest ever built into a commercial airliner. To falter as it had on take-off must have involved failure of at least three and perhaps all four engines. Even with two power plants out, an Electra still can climb like a hawk.

But the odds on seventy-five or a hundred percent engine failure were rated conservatively at one in ten billion. Fuel contamination was another spur-of-the-moment theory but quickly was ruled out.

In Washington, only a few minutes after the Boston accident, Pete Quesada got out of a taxi in front of his house. He had been visiting Russia for a look at Soviet commercial aviation and was glad to get home. In a few seconds he was to wish he had stayed overseas. His wife came racing outside and, almost in tears, blurted:

"Pete, there's been a bad Electra crash!"

"Well, I'll be damned," said Quesada.

He actually was somewhat relieved when he heard the accident had occurred right after take-off.

"I knew structural failure hardly could have been involved in a take-off crash," he said later.

But he also knew it didn't make much difference if an Electra blew a tire while taxiing. No matter what happened to the plane, he was in for it. Senator Hartke's post-Boston crash comment was that he was through with the entire Electra affair. If one more went down, he added, "the blood will be on Quesada's hands."

The FAA chief flew to Boston at six o'clock the following morning. As soon as he landed, he started to enter a car which would take him to a conference with Civil Aeronautics Board officials. Then he spotted a local airport official running toward him, a man Quesada frankly considered a bore.

"Oh God, do I have to cope with this guy now?" he thought.

He told the driver to hurry up, but the official reached the car before it pulled away.

"Pete," he panted, "do you know about the dead birds?"

"I'm worried about dead people, not dead birds," Quesada said testily.

"Pete, come with me. I want to show you something."

Quesada could not help being curious.

"Where are they?" he asked.

"On the runway where the Electra took off," the official replied. "There are hundreds of them."

What happened then is best told in Quesada's own words.

"We drove to the runway, where we got stuck and had to leave the car. We found hundreds of bird carcasses, mostly on the left side of the runway and almost none on the right. I immediately had someone figure out the Eastern Electra's take-off weight and we determined quickly that the plane would have broken ground at just about the point where we found the dead birds.

"We sent for an ornithologist from Harvard who identified the birds as starlings. He told us a starling flock could run into the tens of thousands and that they flew in patterns about one foot apart. This meant one bird for every cubic foot of air. Then we figured out how many cubic feet of air an Allison engine absorbs and what would happen it if were hit by about eight hundred birds every second.

"I knew that a single bird had been known to cause a temporary flame-out (failure) in a turbine engine, so I thought to myself that impact with and subsequent ingestion of a massive bird flock was a reasonable and logical explanation for what had happened.

"Nobody agreed with me at first. I was told that the propeller would have kept birds from entering the engine. But while doing this, the prop also would have kept some air from entering. A witness already had said he saw one of the engines backfiring with a white flash—a good indication of a flame-out.

"I knew people would laugh if I said birds could knock down an Electra. But I communed with myself and decided to announce the bird solution to the press, radio and television."

He did just that—much to the CAB's annoyance. Quesada came right out and said flatly that the Eastern crash was caused by impact with thousands of starlings and that the massive ingestion resulted in multiple engine failure. He explained that a turbine engine will quit at least temporarily if anything disturbs the delicate balance between the mixture of air with fuel.

The CAB was not to issue its findings until nearly two years later. For unlike Quesada, its Bureau of Safety did not buy the bird-ingestion theory right on the spot. Whereas Quesada spoke of a starling mass of between sixty thousand to eighty-four thousand birds, the CAB could find no witness who saw anything closely resembling a flock that size. Quesada said hundreds of bird carcasses were on the left side of the runway. The CAB reported finding exactly seventy-five dead starlings, and thirty of them had been deceased for at least several weeks prior to the accident.

The CAB also was bothered by the results of tests Allison ran in the course of the investigation. The manufacturer fired hundreds of bird carcasses into engines without getting much more than an occasional interruption of power that surged almost immediately back to normal.

It turned out, however, that Quesada's premature solution came pretty close to the truth. Whether he should have announced it when he did—with not much more than circumstantial evidence—is another matter. But he was under an immense strain, and one is tempted to sympathize with his desire to get both the Electra and himself off their latest hook.

The CAB eventually arrived at much the same verdict as Quesada, but with considerable more evidence than a few bird carcasses and some hasty calculations of ingestion effects.

First, it did find indications of bird ingestion in numbers one, two, and four engines, particularly number one, which either had auto-feathered on impact with the starlings or had been feathered manually. Whichever the case, number one lost all power and was not running when the Electra plunged into the harbor.

The other three engines were developing full power at the moment the plane hit the water. But flame-outs or power losses on turbine engines can be very intermittent and momentary. Allison's own tests showed that while the engine could digest birds indefinitely without harm, a particularly heavy ingestion could result in a temporary power loss until the air-fuel mixture was restored to its normal balance.

The CAB was convinced that such a power loss had occurred. There was the witness who had seen a spurt of white flame from number two—exactly what happens in a temporary flame-out. It was likely that number four also had faltered from ingestion.

There was little evidence of ingestion in number three, except for tiny traces of bird feathers in the oil scoop. Working closely with Allison's experts, the CAB deduced this sequence of the Electra's power difficulties:

*Number one*, total loss.

*Number two*, total loss for five to eight seconds before surging back to full power.

*Number three*, may have lost partial power for one or two seconds.

*Number four*, total loss for four to six seconds.

If number three had choked for about as long as a heartbeat, it was easy to figure out what probably happened to the helpless Eastern pilot and his unlucky plane, both trapped in a freakish situation. It was known that at the most critical moment in take-off, he suddenly lost power on three of his four engines. All he had to suffer on his number three power plant was a mere drop of nine hundred revolutions per minute (normal RPMs would hit nearly fourteen thousand) and he would have been without the hydraulic boost mechanism that helps move the controls like automobile power steering.

The Electra's hydraulic system is activated electrically and will operate so long as one engine is functioning normally. In the case of the Boston Electra, the multiple power loss in all four engines would have been the equivalent of turning off the ignition in an automobile and losing all power steering.

Number three, if it did falter for a second, would have reactivated the hydraulic boost as soon as the power surged back to normal. But at this particular moment the pilot was trying to correct the left bank into which the plane had been thrown when both engines on the left side flamed out. This meant he would have been on hard right rudder and full right aileron just when the boost system came back on. The inevitable result: an uncontrolled roll and stall at low altitude from which no recovery was possible.

But suppose number three had *not* lost power, not even for a split second? Then there would have been no difficulty with the hydraulic boost package. This was not only possible but likely, for the CAB found some evidence that the electrical system functioned throughout the fifty-second flight. A surviving stewardess, for example, testified that the cabin lights never went out.

This Electra, however, was doomed whether the pilot had hydraulic boost operative or not. A fully loaded Electra can maintain altitude on only one engine—but it has to be in level flight and at a reasonably high enough altitude. The Eastern plane experienced three-engine power loss on take-off and at exactly the point where the pilot could not trade speed for altitude or altitude for speed. He never got higher than one hundred and forty feet and when trouble hit, he immediately was on the ragged edge of a stall with everything going wrong at once.

There is a little aeronautical fact of life known to pilots as "$V^{mc}$"—velocity-minimum control. In layman's language, the lowest speed at which control of an aircraft can be maintained. Once $V^{mc}$ is violated, a pilot has little control over his airplane through the ailerons, elevators, or rudder. He has only one choice: he must increase flying speed immediately to regain control.

The Eastern pilot had no such choice. If it had been only his number one engine or even numbers one *and* two that faltered, he would have taken instinctive corrective action, namely banking the plane "favorably"—in other words, away from the affected engines—to obtain the necessary speed increase.

Normally an Electra's take-off speed contains a ten percent margin of safety. This means it breaks ground at a speed ten percent higher than $V^{mc}$. Thus even if an engine should fail, there is ample reserve power to continue the climb. But there is a loophole in this margin of safety. The margin exists only (1) when the plane's wings are level, or (2) in the case of single engine failure, when the plane is banked favorably not more than five degrees.

Failure of an outboard engine (numbers one or four) causes an aircraft to bank "unfavorably," in the direction of the dead engine. This causes loss of air speed to such an extent that the minimum speed necessary to maintain control rises sharply. In the Electra, such a circumstance would jump $V^{mc}$ twenty-six knots in the time it would take you to blink your eye. And at Boston, the Eastern Electra suffered not only failure of the number one outboard engine but intermittent loss of power on at least two other engines, all within a space of less than twenty-eight seconds. All the hydraulic boost control aids in the world would not have kept the plane from dropping below $V^{mc}$. It probably never exceeded 120 knots on take-off, and when bird ingestion choked off power, $V^{mc}$ almost instantly rose from 108 knots to at least 134 knots.

The CAB never established whether power was lost on number three. But it did establish, through a series of unusual tests, that it did not make much difference.

The Board borrowed an Electra simulator used by National Airlines for training its Electra crews. Located at Miami, the million-dollar electronic reproduction of the actual airplane is considered the most accurate in existence.

The Board invited sixteen airline captains to Miami. They were not only qualified on Electras but were rated as the best in the country. Each was put into the simulator's left-hand seat, traditional airliner command post, and was told to "take off."

They were not informed, however, what was going to happen on that take-off. The CAB fed into the simulator the probable sequence of events at Boston. First, impact with birds fifty-six feet off the ground. Number one loses all power and auto-feathers. Number two and number four lose all power momentarily. Number three falters just long enough for the electrical system to quit, followed by failure of the boost package, then comes back on.

Every one of the sixteen captains "crashed" the first time the simulated take-off was made. So did the new FAA administrator, Najeeb E. Halaby, himself an able and experienced pilot who was invited to make the same test.

Again, without warning, the CAB fed into the simulator the Boston accident circumstances, but this time with full power on number three. It made little difference. A handful of pilots managed to avoid a crash, but most of them still couldn't keep the simulator under control. All were somewhat shaken by their experience, emerging from the simulator with their shirts sweat-stained.

A total of sixty-six "flights" was made reproducing the Boston accident. Once the guinea-pig pilots knew what to expect, they did better. Captain Charles Ruby of National, for example, crashed the first time, but on his next nine make-believe take-offs he got away safely on five. (Ruby has since become president of the Air Line Pilots Association.)

The Eastern pilot, of course, had had no advance warning. He was exposed to a set of deadly and unprecedented circumstances which he had not been prepared to handle. (One of the beneficial by-products of the Boston accident was extended and improved training in handling Electras exposed to sudden $V^{mc}$ increases in the event of multiple power failure.) And he may have had one further difficulty with which to contend—it was highly likely that he had no indication of air speed when his orderly world began collapsing around him.

The CAB never found the pitot tubes from the Eastern Electra—the tubes through which the passing air stream is directed to the instruments showing air speed. But the Board believes that if the pitot tubes had been located, they probably would have been clogged with bird remains. Such blocking of air passage would have given the pilot a totally false air speed.

Two weeks later another Electra started to take off from Logan and hit a sizable bird flock before it broke ground. The captain aborted take-off and told investigators later that "there wasn't a square inch of my windshield that wasn't splattered with bird remains . . . it was like running into machine-gun fire and I couldn't see a thing."

It would involve no stretching of the imagination to assume that the Eastern pilot had encountered the same destruction of vision. Couple this with his other difficulties. Multiple power failure. Only about ten seconds and ninety feet of altitude in which to decide how to avert disaster. A full eighteen seconds during which he was without sufficient power to maneuver.

The tragedy at Boston can only be summed up as an accident that would not have happened if the triggering device—the initial impact with birds—had occurred five seconds sooner or five seconds later. If the former, he could have aborted. If the latter, he would have been able to continue his climb. He would have had sufficient altitude to put his nose down and pick up speed—and an Electra can climb two hundred and fifty feet a minute even with two engines out.

None of these facts was known at the time of the Eastern crash, however. Quesada's "bird solution," while it tended to take the heat off to some extent, was in itself an unintended further indictment of the Electra. Never before in aviation history had birds caused a fatal crash, although there are bird strikes almost daily.

As a matter of fact, eventual litigation stemming from the accident brought forth a rather startling and totally different explanation. A law firm representing some plaintiffs who had sued Lockheed and Eastern listened very carefully to a theory advanced by a National Airlines captain.

An experienced Electra pilot himself, the captain pointed out that no airman in his right mind would pull back on a control yoke after losing power—it would almost guarantee a stall. He also noted that at least two of the bird-ingested engines had regained power in a matter of seconds, which as far as he was concerned meant the crew still should have been able to maintain level flight and avoid a crash.

Yet the aircraft *had* stalled and he wanted to know why. At his request, the lawyers showed him the plane's maintenance records. The National pilot zeroed in on one apparently insignificant discrepancy: the adjustable right seat occupied by the copilot had a previous history of problems. Six weeks before the Boston accident, the seat had slid backward accidently on two occasions, because of a defective rod. But instead of replacing the entire rod, a mechanic improvised the repairs by using a wire strand shorter than the rod. This makeshift job prevented the seat from locking in place securely; despite further pilot complaints, it was never fixed.

So the National pilot advanced this new theory:

When the bird strike occurred and engine power was lost, the captain must have turned the controls over to the copilot while he tried to ascertain what caused the power loss—this would have been in accordance with emergency procedures established by many airlines, including Eastern at the time.

The copilot was now flying the plane. Attempting to correct the sudden yaw to the left, he hits the right rudder pedal so hard that the defective seat slides backward and his foot leaves the pedal. Instinctively he grabs at the yoke trying to bring the seat forward—and the nose goes up . . .

The CAB's official causal findings were never reversed, even after this new explanation was cited during the litigation proceedings. Yet not a few safety experts agreed with the defective seat theory, as far-fetched as it might seem. Perhaps if it had been pursued more diligently by the CAB, the Electra wouldn't have taken another beating in both press and Congress—and Electra bashing was very much in fashion.

Shortly after the crash at Logan, a House of Representatives subcommittee opened hearings on the entire Electra problem amid renewed Congressional demands for grounding. And birds or no birds, this time there was some widespread editorial pressure for grounding, too, even though there was not one shred of evidence to connect the Eastern accident with Tell City or Buffalo.

Included among the hearing witnesses were a number of Braniff officials and pilots. The very day they were testifying as to the company's confidence in the Electra, Braniff filed a four and a half million dollar suit against Lockheed, charging design negligence.

The suit, similar to one filed later by Northwest, merely was Braniff's legal attempt to recover the entire cost of the plane lost at Buffalo plus a cushion against the lawsuits being filed against the airline itself. But the incongruity of accusing Lockheed of poor design at the very moment Braniff was defending the airplane before Congress did not exactly reassure the public.

Despite the bird explanation, it was obvious that the Boston accident had stirred up old fears and prejudices. The average passenger, who knew little if anything about such things as whirl mode, fail-safe, flutter, diagonal bracings, wing ribs, ingestion, or hydraulic boost units, was only aware that another Electra had crashed, killing more people. In fact, there was a general feeling that if mere birds could knock a huge airliner out of the sky, it must be unsafe, period. What was being accomplished in LEAP, being highly technical, meant little to the layman. One fatal crash obliterated all the official assurances about the Electra.

The subcommittee hearings reflected the reborn concern. Under the direction of Mississippi's John Bell Williams, a former pilot himself and a congressman with a

solid and objective grasp of aviation problems, they were
directed mainly at determining the plane's over-all safety.

The inquiry was impressive on one particular score. It
was expected that Lockheed, Allison, and the Electra-
operating airlines would defend the airplane. But the
witnesses scoring the most points were pilots, hammering
away on two main themes:

First, crews still were bidding Electra trips in preference to piston-engine planes. Second, pilots would not fly
a transport they considered unsafe.

"I would actually regret having to return to one of our
piston-engine aircraft, and all of the pilots I have talked to
who have flown the Electra feel the same way," said
Captain Trooper Shaw of Braniff.

Representing the Air Line Pilots Association directly
and Eastern indirectly was Captain Edward J. Bechtold, a
big, handsome veteran not only of airline flying but of
accident investigation. He had participated in the Buffalo
and Tell City probes as well as Boston. Bechtold was and
is one of those dedicated men who give the lie to the
charge that the average airline pilot thinks only of getting
more money for less on-duty time than any other profes-
sion in the world. If he ever had been compensated financially for the hours he has spent on air safety projects and
investigations, he could have retired long ago as a wealthy
man.

Bechtold told the subcommittee that what he was about
to say represented information garnered from more than
one thousand pilots flying the Electra. He pointed out that
evidence on the Boston crash still was being sifted and
that his remarks were directed to the Electra's safety in
general.

"First," said Bechtold, "while we believe that the modification program under way at the Lockheed plant is certain to strengthen the wing and engine mount structure of
the aircraft, we would not want to leave the impression

that the modification alone will absolutely preclude future
accidents from occurring to the Electra."

The subcommittee stirred uneasily.

"It has been said," Bechtold continued calmly, "that
aviation is not inherently dangerous, but that—like the
sea—it is awfully unforgiving of mistakes, whether they
occur as a result of the person manipulating the controls,
or on the drawing board of the design engineer, or during
the installation of a component by a mechanic. The net
result can be, and frequently is, catastrophic.

"While the ALPA Electra Evaluation Committee sub-
scribes to the Electra as being one of the finest airplanes
which we have ever flown, it—like other aircraft—has
some features on which improvement can be made. These,
in our opinion, do not make the Electra any less satisfactory for airline service than any one of the other twelve or
fourteen transports in current use."

The subcommittee stopped stirring.

Bechtold went on to elaborate on some of the areas in
which pilots felt the Electra could be improved, but emphasized that none had any connection with the Buffalo or
Tell City accident.

Bechtold then quoted from previous ALPA reports on
those two crashes and the subsequent LEAP program:

"The ALPA representatives have had the benefit of
conferences with the most responsible people in Lockheed,
FAA and NASA, and are of the opinion that the Electra
can be safely flown under the present operating restrictions, bearing in mind conscientious compliance with all
inspection and good operating practices.

"ALPA representatives . . . have become convinced that
the fixes being incorporated in the Electra will eliminate
the possibility of an unbalanced engine or propeller combination from driving the nacelle or the wing to a point
where either will become detached from the airplane.
[Only a pilot or engineer could refer to catastrophic flutter
in such delicate, unfrightening language!] The strength

built into the Electra is such that an unbalanced condition in the engine and propeller will result in the separation of the propeller rather than in disintegration of the aircraft structure. It is our viewpoint that Lockheed has made conscientious, thorough efforts to investigate all possible malfunctions of the Electra which might have been attributable to the Buffalo or Tell City accidents. When Project LEAP is complete, it is our opinion that the aircraft will be structurally capable of resuming its design speed as a safe and efficient air carrier airplane."

Having read those two pilot verdicts, Bechtold added his own.

"It is obvious," he said quietly, "that the aviation industry has benefited from these investigations into the Electra problems. We believe the advancement in prevention of flutter is of a similar magnitude to the extensive advancement made in preventing explosive decompression following the series of accidents to the DeHavilland Comet."

(He was referring to the pioneering British jetliner which was grounded after three of them blew up. The Comet's original and since corrected weakness was inexperience in high speed, high-altitude cabin pressurization that led to premature metal fatigue. The lessons learned from these accidents have been applied to every jet transport built since the Comet.)

The subcommittee, impressed by the solid industry-government-pilot support of the Electra, did not recommend grounding. And throughout the country spontaneous pilot defense of the plane began sprouting at the least sign of unfavorable comment. Typical was a letter sent to the editor of a Miami newspaper which had published an editorial urging that the Electra be grounded because of the Boston crash. The writer was Captain Dick Merrill of Eastern, who had been flying since the days of wood-and-fabric airplanes.

"First," he wrote, "no pilot is required to fly any airplane if he has any question of its airworthiness. He has two yardsticks to measure that: (A) all the knowledge he has accumulated in a lifetime of flying, plus a thorough technical knowledge of the particular airplane; and (B) even more exacting, most pilots I know ask themselves whether they would take their wives, children, and mothers in that airplane with them.

"Second, any captain or pilot eligible to fly the Electra has enough seniority to choose any type of aircraft he wants to fly. My choice, and that of scores of my associates, is the Electra."

George Carroll, veteran aviation editor of the New York *Journal-American*, went to a highly reliable source for an opinion on the Electra's safety—Clarence N. Sayen, president of ALPA at that time.

"Members wouldn't be flying the Electra today if they didn't consider it a safe airplane," Sayen told Carroll. "Our fellows just wouldn't be up there on the flight deck if they thought there was anything wrong with the ship."

American Airlines circularized a letter among the 44,000 members of its Admirals' Club, an informal organization consisting mostly of customers who fly American frequently. Signed by Thornton Wagner, the airline's chief engineering test pilot, it again hammered away on the theme that the Electra was a "pilot's airplane," loved by virtually every man who ever flew it.

Load factors continued to be depressed during the next few weeks after Boston. American Airlines ran a survey covering traffic in eleven cities—New York, Rochester, Philadelphia, Buffalo, Washington, Boston, Detroit, Chicago, St. Louis, Dallas, and Cincinnati—over a ten-day period following the Logan crash. It revealed that 2298 passengers in those cities canceled or refused reservations on the airline's Electras, giving the Boston accident as the specific reason!

But despite this setback, the barrage of pro-Electra arguments was beginning to take effect. It was not readily discernible at this stage, but the black eye was beginning to fade.

## 8

# Comeback

Slowly, gradually, the Electra fought its way back into public confidence. Considering the enormity of its troubles and the abuse that had been heaped upon it, the comeback was nothing short of miraculous. One could have gotten rich if he had received five dollars for every time it was said "the Electra is finished as a commercial transport." And it was a remark made by a cross section of American aviation—government officials, industry executives, airline people.

The plane itself was partially responsible for making hash out of the gloomy predictions. It had been designed for passenger comfort, and its virtues in that respect finally began emerging from the shadows of its ravaged reputation. The memories of Buffalo and Tell City faded, it was obvious that the Boston crash had had nothing to do with the aircraft's structural integrity, and Lockheed's Burbank assembly line, manned by five thousand workers, inspectors, and engineers, was rolling out a fully modified Electra at a rate of better than one a day.

Like forgiving parents embracing a sinning daughter, the airlines once more began mentioning the fact that they were flying Electras. They even came up with new names for the modified version. "Electra II" it was called by American, Braniff, and others. Eastern and Pacific Southwest advertised the "Super Electra."

One carrier in particular defended the plane not only after modification was well under way but even in the dark days of rumors, dwindling loads, and open passenger resistance. That was American, which not only waged a brilliant defensive battle but took the offensive.

American president C. R. Smith called a meeting of the airline's top brass. Every man crammed into C. R.'s relatively small office had already read copies of a confidential report Bill Littlewood had received from Lockheed on the progress of the investigation. Its gist was that Lockheed was almost sure of what was wrong with the Electra, that it was serious enough to require mammoth and lengthy modifications, but that the plane could continue to operate safely under its current speed restrictions.

Smith asked every officer present if, based on that report, he considered the Electra safe to fly and the manufacturer's proposed "fix" program feasible. The response was unanimously affirmative.

C. R. leaned back in his chair and announced, "All right, we'll keep 'em flying." He turned to Willis Player, vice president of public relations. "And it's your job, Willis, to persuade the public they're safe."

It was Player who organized a second meeting, this one secret, shortly after the Boston crash. Attending were the top officials of all seven U.S. domestic airlines flying Electras. And it was Smith who proposed to his peers the organization of "fact teams" that would tour the nation and resell the maligned airliner to press and public.

The heated discussion that followed his suggestion was reminiscent of that hectic meeting Quesada had held at the FAA following Tell City. Some of the airlines argued that a frontal attack was a waste of time and money, that it would be best to let time take its course and hope that the public eventually would forget what had happened.

C. R., with nearly ninety million dollars tied up in an Electra fleet that was flying half empty too often, said in effect, the hell with hiding heads in the sand, this still was a damned good airplane, so let's go out and fight all the phony rumors and grounding demands.

His competitors, some of them with open reluctance, finally agreed to furnish American's fact teams with supporting personnel, especially pilots. On November 1, 1960, the first of five "truth squads" began the most unusual crusade in aviation annals. It included Bill Littlewood, who could have explained the construction of an atomic bomb in logical, simple terms to a grammar school student. He headed the initial team. Other members included American's personable vice-president for public relations, Willis Player; Captain Art Weidman, a seventeen-year veteran with American; Captain Warren Schultz of Northwest; and Captain Jack Isbill of National.

The team hit New York, Washington, and Chicago on its first swing. It not only held news conferences, but briefed local civic groups, met with congressmen, and even submitted to searching question-and-answer sessions with airline sales and operating personnel.

Each meeting followed a set pattern. Littlewood opened by reading a statement of policy signed by Smith.

"We operate American Airlines," the statement declared, "on the basis that *we* are responsible for the safety of our passengers. While the Federal Aviation Agency has equal responsibility and equal determination to have safety in air transportation, we consider the basic obligation to provide a safe operation to be our own, and we are responsible for our judgment and our decisions.

"The good reputation of American Airlines is more valuable than the property rights in a fleet of airplanes. If we believed the Electra to be unsafe, we would ground it."

Littlewood followed with a discussion of the Electra's history, the causes of the Buffalo and Tell City crashes and explanation of the "fix," assurance that the other three accidents involving Electras (Boston and the two at La Guardia) could have happened to any airplane, and finally a solemn declaration that with the speed restrictions, the Electra was as safe as any airliner flying.

Weidman, an earnest and persuasive man in his sincerity, gave the pilots' view. Then the team opened the meeting to questions—and not a single one was left unanswered and dangling in vagueness or evasions.

In two months the five fact teams covered eighteen of the twenty-six major cities served by Electras. *Flying's* Lou Davis, surveying the results of the unprecedented campaign, wrote:

"The program delivered many side benefits in addition to clearing the air on the Electra story. It brought American closer to the passenger and fortified its own personnel with confidence, producing answers to questions on which they themselves may have nursed secret concern."

American did not stop with the fact teams. It took out of mothballs a confidence-winning gimmick almost as old as air travel itself—the sightseeing flight. At New York, Chicago, and Washington, it offered a thirty-minute ride in an Electra for $6.50 and aimed its advertising at two categories: first-timers and those who feared the Electra.

The response surprised even the American officials who thought up the idea. Stewardesses passed out questionnaires asking each passenger why he had taken the flight. A whopping fifty percent replied that they had never flown before and were just curious.

The sightseeing flights turned out to be airborne parties. Children were given junior-pilot and stewardess wings. Picture taking was encouraged. Every person aboard received American promotion material, including brochures on the Electra. Scale-model Electra kits were awarded youngsters guessing closest on the plane's current speed and altitude. The popularity of the flights was so overwhelming that they were extended to Boston, Nashville, Syracuse, Buffalo, Detroit, Hartford, and Philadelphia.

American's market research revealed that many businessmen, while unconcerned about the Electra, were avoiding it because their wives expressed concern. The airline invited one of the nation's leading woman pilots, Jerrie Cobb, to fly the plane—figuring if it were publicized that a mere woman could handle it, wives might change their minds about the Electra.

Not by any stretch of the imagination could Jerrie Cobb be called a "mere woman." She held numerous aviation speed records, was the first of her sex to pass astronaut physical tests, worked for Aero Commander as advertising and sales promotion manager, and had no less than eight thousand hours of flight time logged. But up to the day she sat down in the left seat of an Electra flight deck, she had never seen the inside of its cockpit, let alone flown the big transport.

American invited this writer along on the flight. I sat nervously in the jump seat while Art Weidman briefed Miss Cobb, an exceptionally attractive, pony-tailed blonde, on take-off procedures. But anyone who went along on the hop would have had to modify his opinion of women drivers, or even women pilots.

Weidman had her doing forty-five-degree banks, standing the Electra on one wing. He tested her ability to recover from stalls. She made three landings and by the third was setting the Electra down so gently that she wouldn't have cracked an eggshell glued to the landing gear.

At 8000 feet Weidman chopped the power on three engines. The air speed dropped only slightly, and the altimeter didn't lose one foot.

On one take-off, Weidman killed an engine just as the ship broke ground. It climbed as if nothing had happened. On the next, Weidman told Miss Cobb to leave the throttles at full power after the Electra was airborne. The plane hit 4000 feet in about sixty seconds.

The demonstration was so impressive that I asked Weidman if I could fly it.

"Sure," Weidman grinned.

I set my jaw as John Wayne would do under similar circumstances. My flying technique had all the stability of a pogo stick, but the Electra handled docilely and uncomplainingly. Between Miss Cobb and this far less experienced "birdman" the Electra proved it is the easiest transport to fly since the DC-3.

Arthur Godfrey also flew an American Electra and reported to his sizable audience that nobody should be afraid to ride the prop-jet "any time it's available."

The new Federal Aviation Agency administrator, Najeeb E. Halaby, who had not been involved in the Electra controversy, put an Electra through a grueling test flight shortly after he was appointed to succeed Quesada. Halaby, an ex-Lockheed test pilot, announced after the flight that "I wouldn't hesitate to have my family travel in Electras."

By April, 1961, nearly half the one hundred and sixty Electras in airline service throughout the world had moved down the Burbank modification line. It took twenty days

*DC-3*

per aircraft, with nine being worked on simultaneously. First, a stripping process with the engines, nacelles, wing tips, and leading wing edges removed. Stripped parts were carefully packaged, marked, and stocked for reinstallation if no modification was required.

The nacelles were moved to a separate modification line, where the additional structure and engine support mountings were incorporated. Each aircraft was moved on a set of jigs strong enough to keep the entire plane, fuselage, and wings from any distortion as it rolled down the line. The calculated tolerance of movement was only 6/1000 of an inch.

The first step after stripping equipment was removal of the old wing planks and preparing for installation of new ribs. Since all of the ribs inboard of the aileron were to be replaced, every other one was worked on to maintain structural wing shape during the modification process. When half were so completed, workers went back and replaced the remainder.

Certain autopilot revisions ordered by FAA were handled in the field, with Lockheed supplying a "kit" at no cost. It was made available long before LEAP got well under way, enabling the airlines to incorporate the improved autopilots in unmodified Electras.

By the end of September, 1961, two years after Buffalo, Texas, not only was LEAP completed but also the Electra's comeback. Carrier by carrier reported this dramatic evidence:

American—Electra load factors were averaging higher than the pure jets.

Northwest—from April, 1960 (one month after Tell City) through July of the same year, Electra load factors averaged only fifty-six percent. In the same period in 1961, they climbed to more than sixty-three percent. By September they were surpassing Northwest's plush DC-8s and proven DC-6Bs and DC-7s. Only Northwest's brandnew Boeing 720s were turning in better load factors.

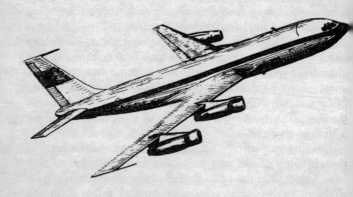

*Boeing 720*

Western—In January, 1960, Electra load factors hit an all-time high of nearly seventy-eight percent. By the following June, they had slumped to forty-nine percent. In August of 1961, they had climbed back to sixty-two percent.

Braniff—Electra load factors in the fall of '61 were running neck and neck with Boeing 707s, representing an incredible fifty percent increase over the spring of 1960.

Eastern and National reported similar improvement. National, in fact, had an increase of nearly seventy percent in revenue passenger miles between July, 1959, and July, 1961, and attributed much of it to the Electra's comeback.

Little but lively Pacific Southwest was so pleased with its four Electras that it decided to do something special on the occasion of the delivery of its fifth, ten days ahead of schedule. It took one hundred and eighty Lockheed production workers on three-hour courtesy flights, complete with refreshments. The "Thank the Builder" gesture was the first of its kind in the history of the aircraft industry.

Not even two unfortunate events in 1961 kept the Electra from its comeback course.

In February of that year, when LEAP's modification program was in full swing, the Federal Aviation Agency found it necessary to fine Lockheed $6000 for sloppy assembly-line practices. Specifically, Eastern found a rivet gun, twenty screws, a small vacuum cleaner, and a piece of paper cup in the wing tanks of two Electras during an inspection while the planes were undergoing modification. American had minor bolts missing from various sections of no fewer than thirteen of its Electras. Western reported finding trash in one wing tank.

The FAA could have socked Lockheed with a maximum $17,000 penalty, but reduced the fine to $6000 when the embarrassed company took drastic corrective action. It put specially trained mechanics, wearing pocketless coveralls, on the assembly line, installed rigid inventories of all material going into open wings and tanks, and added a special final inspection process.

"We had no excuse, no alibi, no extenuating circumstances to fall back on," a Lockheed official admitted later with admirable frankness. "We just assumed our inspection checks were pretty damned good and we found out they were a long way from being as good as they should have been."

In truth, Lockheed's misdeeds were more of the redface than black-mark variety. The assembly-line carelessness in no way compromised the safety of the airplanes involved, and Lockheed's experience was typical of similar worker forgetfulness that has plagued automobile and airplane production lines for years. There is an unconfirmed but widely believed yarn that has been floating around the airline industry for a long time concerning a mysterious rattle that kept occurring above the cabin of a brand-new airliner. Mechanics finally opened the ceiling lining and found an empty soft-drink bottle flopping around inside.

The second incident was far more serious. On September 17 a Northwest Electra took off from Chicago's O'Hare Airport, rolled over on one wing, and crashed. It never got higher than two hundred feet. All thirty-seven aboard perished in an accident that was alarmingly reminiscent of the Boston crash—with no birds to blame this time.

But unlike Boston, in the Northwest tragedy the pilot was able to supply a key clue before he and his passengers died—the tape recording of his air-tower communication. He had taken off in normal fashion and started a gentle right turn shortly after breaking ground. Instead of straightening, however, the Electra kept tightening its turn until it ran out of sky. After much deciphering difficulty, experts finally discovered that the pilot's final transmission revealed some kind of control trouble.

The recording of that last message was less than eight seconds in duration. The rapid voice, the short phrasing, and the high pitch were typical of a man under great stress.

". . . [static] We're in trouble . . . uh . . . all units holding . . . [static] . . . Northwest Electra, I still don't have (or get) release . . . right turn in . . . no control."

"No control."

Autopilot malfunction? The autopilot had been placarded inoperative because it had not yet been modified in accordance with the LEAP program.

Asymmetrical flaps—a condition in which flap retraction is uneven? The Electra has a switch which automatically evens the flaps if they vary as little as two degrees. Even if the switch does not function, a pilot can override a balky flap.

Aileron trouble? The ailerons are used to turn and bank an aircraft. The Northwest plane obviously had been locked in a right turn. And investigators, concentrating on the ailerons, quickly found something amiss. Fracture marks on the right aileron showed it was jammed before impact, locked in a six-degree variance from normal.

The CAB's inquiry disclosed that six weeks before the accident, Northwest's routine maintenance of this particular Electra had called for changing the hydraulic boost package. To remove this package, it was necessary to disconnect a safety wire which gave the aileron cable exactly the right tension during an upward movement.

Three separate shifts of mechanics had worked on the plane during this overhaul period. The CAB found the mechanic who had disconnected the safety wire, but it never could find one who could say positively that he had put it back.

Because the cable was never resafetied, eventually it worked loose and caused the aileron to jam in a turn. From such outwardly insignificant human errors, from such fleeting moments of carelessness, are born air disasters.

The industry held its collective breath after the latest Electra mishap. But there was little backwash of public resistance to the plane, no sign of new fears. Some airlines reported a temporary drop in load factors. Others had none. It was just another accident, and the Electra by now had achieved the ultimate in vindication. It was just another airliner, subject to the same vagaries of fate and human folly as any other plane.

It also was a plane that in efficient, economical performance of its job seemed to be trying to atone for its past sins. Throughout 1961, Electras operated by U.S. airlines consistently led all other types in on-time performance— which by CAB standards means arrivals and departures within fifteen minutes of schedule. In this department they were regularly surpassing even the pure jets, even though Electra trips generally were shorter and frequently involved multiple stops. By June of 1962, American was reporting Electra maintenance reliability as the best in its fleet, along with the highest load factors.

Foreign carriers reported the same experience. The

Netherlands' KLM, which bought twelve Electras, pronounced them the most popular plane in the fleet for these reasons:

—As in this country, they were delivering the best on-time figures, not only on a current basis but beating any plane in KLM's history.

—Maintenance costs were running fifteen percent below budget estimates.

—In the winter of 1960, Electras serving the Moscow run turned in a better regularity record than pure jets operating over the same route.

—In the last three months of 1960, Electras had fewer than three delays of more than one hour for every one hundred hours flown, a record not only twice as good as that of all other KLM aircraft, but the best performance of any KLM plane in the airline's forty-two-year existence.

Foreign airlines flying Electras had observed the same speed restrictions applied to this country's carriers, with the same economic results. KLM alone admitted losing two million dollars in 1960 from a combination of slumping load factors and increased operating expenses. But the comeback cycle applied overseas, too, and by mid-1961 the Electra was back in good graces wherever it flew.

When LEAP was finished in the summer of that year, the one hundred and sixty Electras serving fourteen airlines had logged more than six hundred thousand hours' flight time, enough for about seven thousand trips around the world or nearly seventy-five thousand flights between Los Angeles and New York. Electras were making forty-three hundred scheduled flights weekly and more than six hundred daily. In fact, an Electra was landing or taking off every seventy seconds, twenty-four hours a day and seven days a week.

The comeback was especially heartening to the man who had had the most faith in the plane as well as the greatest stake in it. That was Robert E. Gross, Lockheed's board chairman. But tragedy finally touched him, as it had touched his proudest product.

On September 3, 1961, Bob Gross died in a Santa Monica hospital of cancer. He was sixty-four. His younger brother, Courtlandt Gross, succeeded him as board chairman.

In three decades Gross had built the firm into the nation's twenty-eighth-largest industrial concern, a manufacturing giant that had written aviation history. There were the sleek speedsters of the thirties that gave the infant industry new standards of safety, performance, and reliability. There was the P-38, a World War II fighter dreaded by every Japanese pilot who encountered one. There was the Constellation, first of the postwar airliners and the plane that introduced transatlantic travel to millions. There was the F-80, America's first operational jet fighter. There was the T-33, the Air Force's first jet trainer.

*P-38 "Lightning"*

But his pet, his favorite, always was the first Electra, the doughty little transport that really put Lockheed into commercial aviation.

Even his only granddaughter had been named Electra.

*F-80*

# 9

# Aftermath

The most frequent question asked about the Electra is whether it now is a safe airplane. The answer must be a positive, unequivocal yes; or the highest aviation officials in the federal government, more than one thousand Electra-qualified airline captains, some of the nation's finest scientific brains, the engineers of two fine corporations, and the top personnel of fourteen airlines throughout the world are guilty at best of self-delusion or at worst, outright fabrication of the facts. No stronger statement can be written. It would not have been written, for that matter, if the author had not been personally convinced of its truth after eighteen months of research into the Electra story, during the course of which I talked to many persons who did not and still do not like the plane, as well as those who loved it and always will.

The second most frequent question is who was responsible for two of aviation's most terrible crashes. To this, there is no positive answer and there may never be. The area of responsibility is neither black nor white. It is composed of conflict, emotion, and contradiction.

For a long time the two parties most concerned—Lockheed and Allison—kept insisting that Buffalo and Tell City were "state of the art" accidents. The unfortunate, tragic product of inexperience and innocent assumptions concerning flutter.

Robert E. Gross told the House subcommittee investigating the Electra in November of 1960:

"I know it is disturbing to many people and perhaps to you how highly competent and old-line aircraft companies can turn out planes which after a few months of service experience difficulties. The art of aircraft design has grown rapidly and in spurts from the days of the earliest rudimentary machines to the present-day planes requiring hundreds of thousands of man-hours of engineering design, wind-tunnel testing, and flying.

"New and complicated problems arise with each generation of aircraft, requiring an ever-increasing volume of analyses and tests to assure safety. Sometimes, however, it is just not possible to foresee the almost infinite variety of combinations of circumstances that can affect an airplane in flight.

"The two Electra accidents in Texas and Indiana resulted from conditions that were not disclosed in the thousands of tests to which the Electra was subjected. They were unpredictable within the then-existing state of the art. It is some consolation to realize that the state of the art has advanced as the result of our findings."

By the spring of 1962, however, a total of *fifty-five million dollars* in lawsuits had been filed against Lockheed, Allison, Braniff, and Northwest by relatives of those who died at Buffalo and Tell City. "State of the art" offered no solid legal defense against this courtroom onslaught, even though it happened to come closer to the truth than any other explanation. The result was a bitter battle between the two corporate giants, Lockheed and the Allison division of General Motors, over who was to blame.

Under this heavy financial threat, Lockheed abandoned its "state of the art" stand and waded into Allison.

On April 14, 1962, Lockheed for the first time charged openly that the deadly whirl mode had been triggered at both Buffalo and Tell City by an in-flight break in the propeller-reduction gearbox, which, as reported previously, was a key part of the engine. The fatigue crack, Lockheed said, began a chain of failure in the Braniff number one and Northwest number four engines that literally broke the power plants in two. This, Lockheed continued, provided the "play" necessary to start the propellers wobbling and eventually resulted in destructive flutter.

Lockheed's new analysis of the two accidents included these key assertions:

—Fatal whirl mode cannot be transmitted to a wing through just a weakened nacelle. Thus whirl mode is possible only if a failure within the engine itself occurs first.

—In both crashes, the gearbox and power sections of both suspect engines were found widely separated on the ground, indicating in-flight separation rather than damage from impact.

—Pieces of those engines showed marks of broken engine parts that had battered each other during whirl mode. This could have happened only if the airframe remained sound enough to hold the engine components together until flutter broke the wings.

—The Braniff and Northwest suspect engines showed fatigue breaks in the gearbox casings virtually identical to fatigue cracks experienced by an Australian airline on two of its Electras in 1960, by the military on four Allison engines similar to the commercial version, and by Allison itself on a test stand.

—The engine, not the nacelle, must have been broken because tests were run which showed that to transmit the whirl mode and its associated forces, the nacelle would have to be intact to serve as a transmission link. In other words, had the nacelle been weakened, it would not have been possible for these high loads to be transferred back through the wing if the link was not intact.

The engine manufacturer fired a counterblast that not only denied Lockheed's charges but even cast some serious doubt on the entire whirl mode theory.

Declared Allison:

—The fatigue cracks that occurred in the gearbox casings of the two Australian Electras were detected from oil seepage, something that did not appear in the maintenance records of the Braniff and Northwest planes. The Australian carrier's incidents involved engines that had not been modified to correct an admitted tendency toward fatigue breaks found and corrected in subsequent development testing. Braniff's and Northwest's engines *had* been modified.

—The fractures which Lockheed claimed were caused by fatigue actually showed definite evidence of instantaneous failure from abnormal flight loads. Allison's own tests demonstrated that the modified gearbox casings were twice as strong as needed to withstand nacelle failure.

—Further Allison tests proved that the struts connecting the gearbox to the power section were buckled or bowed in such a way that the damage could have resulted solely from an airframe breaking up.

—Some of the engine damage cited by Lockheed as proof that gearbox failure ignited whirl mode was identical to the damage found in the engines of the Northwest Electra that crashed at Chicago—and that accident did *not* involve the flutter phenomenon

—Lockheed's whirl mode theory assumes misalignment of the propeller shaft by at least ten degrees. Yet even distortion of only two and a half degrees would have brought the rear of the prop spinner into contact with the engine cowl. There was no such contact damage found.

Allison's own verdict was that the engine damage mostly resulted from violent loads originating *outside* the power plants. And Allison's explanation of Buffalo and Tell City discounted whirl mode. It pinned the former on a high speed dive following autopilot failure. It pinned the latter on separation of the wing from abnormal, clear-air turbulence loads. Why, Allison argued, should whirl mode have destroyed two Electras when other planes using the same engine encountered no such difficulty?

There was only one implication to be drawn. Namely, that Allison felt the Electra wing was marginal to begin with. Allison engineers charged that in January of 1959, after the Electra had gone into service, a Lockheed official came to Indianapolis and told them, "We're in trouble. We've got high stresses on the outboards."

They said further that it was then planned to pull one of American's new Electras out of service for inspection of the outboards. The plane designated was the one that crashed in New York's East River before inspection could be made.

"We were scared to death the accident involved structural failure," recalls one Allison official, "but it turned out to be something else and everyone relaxed."

According to Allison, the Electra barely passed the old CAA's flutter-resistant standards—and then only by reducing the maximum permissible fuel load in the outboard wing sections, which the CAA figured would be consumed in taxiing.

"The Electra," charged one top Allison engineer, "was approved in good faith but the margin for error was too slim."

Was the original wing too weak? In the course of researching this book, the author was told by one government official that the Lockheed engineer who designed the wing wanted a stronger structure but was overruled because it would have cut the plane's speed capacity.

Allison itself claimed that of the twenty-five million dollars spent on LEAP, seventeen million went into wing strengthening—which to the engine manufacturer was proof that wing design and not whirl mode was at the root of the Electra's troubles.

Both these statements, the alleged overruling of a designer and LEAP's apparently greater concentration on the wing than on the nacelle structure, were discussed frankly with Lockheed vice-president J. F. (Jerry) McBrearty. His answers:

"The story of the overruled designer is totally false. First of all, no one person designs a wing structure. The design process is a constant series of consultations and decisions involving a number of designers and structures experts. Time after time during the design process the stress men question a design decision and call for either greater or lesser strength than the designer had provided for a given component. From the beginning, the Electra met or exceeded the strength levels specified by the CAA in every area. It is Lockheed's position that the forces set up in whirl mode were so severe, they would have failed a wing made of cast iron.

"As for LEAP's dollar amounts, the exact figures are not significant. The point is that the nacelle work and the wing job were not related. The nacelle and engine work was done to prevent the phenomenon of whirl mode from happening again; in short, to prevent repetition of the accidents. The wing work was an improvement to assure long fatigue life and prevent damage after long service with the airplane. It was an improvement that simply was found to be desirable as a by-product of the investigation and was done as a bonus during the LEAP modification."

Perhaps more important than "Who goofed?" is "Did they fix it?" On that score, Lockheed and Allison were in complete agreement but for different reasons. Lockheed because it asserted that the nacelle-engine structure had been corrected, making whirl mode impossible; Allison because the Electra wing had been beefed up.

One of the saddest developments in the Electra story was the feud between the two companies, both splendid examples of American industrial skill and integrity. It is not within this writer's own technological knowledge to pass judgment on which was guilty and which was innocent, or whether both were culpable to some extent. Lockheed's attempt to tag Allison with the responsibility for Buffalo and Tell City and Allison's counterattack were made public *after* the CAB issued its findings on the accidents.

In fairness to Lockheed, these findings gave whirl mode as the probable cause, but did not or could not say definitely what "prior damage" triggered it. In fairness to Allison, these findings absolved the reduction gearbox as the triggering source. And perhaps the real answer lies in an answer Lockheed's McBrearty gave to the author when he was asked, "Why did it happen?"

"You have to go back to the fail-safe concept which was aimed largely at structural integrity," McBrearty replied thoughtfully. "There always have been areas in which this concept was not considered necessary. Like the Comet and the twin problem of pressurization and metal fatigue. That resulted in application of fail-safe to those two areas in every turbine-powered plane built since then, including the Electra. In the case of the Electra, we learned the

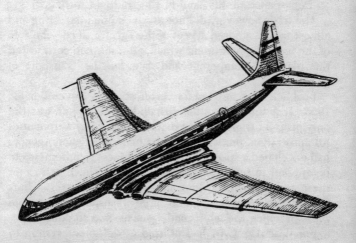

*Comet*

hard way that the fail-safe philosophy also was necessary in flutter prevention."

In effect, his answer added up to a "state of the art" explanation. What LEAP accomplished was extension of the fail-safe concept to the Electra's nacelle and wing structure, which seems to be the most objective comment that can be made on the subject.

On February 12, 1962, Lockheed and Allison began presenting their conflicting views in a Houston, Texas, courtroom. The occasion was the trial of a $500,000 lawsuit brought by the family of one of the Buffalo crash victims.

Two months later, the jury brought in the verdict. It awarded the family $250,000 in damages and found Lockheed and Allison equally responsible. It held that both companies were jointly involved in the Electra's engine-mounting design. It found negligence in the overall design of the aircraft and its power plants, in engine-airframe compatibility, and in Electra flight testing.

The trial, however, did not dwell on one interesting and almost totally ignored aspect of the Electra story—the role of the federal government which, after all, had certificated the plane as competent and safe for the transport of passengers

Lockheed had applied for certification on November 11, 1955, at a time when the British-built Viscount was the only prop-jet transport in existence. The Civil Aeronautics Administration, predecessor of the Federal Aviation Agency, had developed a special set of airworthiness requirements to be applied to turbine-powered airliners. The Electra met these requirements, which included ability to resist flutter. But there still was one large unsuspected loophole through which the whirl-mode menace was to pour.

For years the CAA had utilized a "designee" system to assure compliance with its regulations. Under this system, key employees of the applicant manufacturer were delegated to approve test methods and data, blueprints, design work, etc. The perennially money-starved CAA simply did not have the manpower to monitor aircraft design. Theoretically it was supposed to approve design analysis, but in actual practice it was the manufacturer who did all the work and passed virtually all the judgment. The CAA administrator merely reviewed the data before issuing a type certificate.

This system, with its tragically obvious weaknesses, had caused trouble long before the Electra came along. The Civil Air Regulations specifically prohibited the CAA administrator from certificating any airliner with a feature or characteristic that would make it unsafe for the transport category. Yet three planes—the DC-6, the Constellation, and the Martin 202—all received certificates in spite of design deficiencies that were in open violation of the CAA's own regulations!

On the DC-6, the CAA approved the location of the cabin heater air-intake scoop almost directly behind a fuel-dumping vent for an alternate wing tank. The regulations specifically stated that "it shall not be possible for fuel to flow between tanks in quantity sufficient to cause an overflow . . . vents and drainage shall not terminate at points where the discharge of fuel shall constitute a fire hazard."

Fifty-two persons died when a United DC-6, engaged in a fuel transfer from one tank to another, caught fire and crashed—because in the course of the transfer, gas overflowed and was sucked into the cabin heater. Douglas caught the blame and it was United and American who suffered through a subsequent costly grounding. But there were no damage suits filed against the federal government. Nor was there any public outcry against the United States Congress, which for years treated the CAA like an unwanted stepchild, ignoring the warnings of the entire aviation industry that the lifeblood of commercial aviation was adequate research and enforcement funds.

Lockheed and every airline using its new Constellations

were the parties that paid for a fatal crash stemming from a poorly designed electrical system—one approved by the CAA like a blindly applied rubber stamp. Ditto the Martin 202, with a wing weakness so obvious that the CAB, investigating a fatal Martin crash, could not believe the CAA had even looked at the design of the key structural part which failed.

Aircraft designers are as prone to human error as pilots. Congress wrote into law, as a safeguard against such mistakes, a federal inspection-and-approval system and then—as it had done once before in a little experiment known as Prohibition—neglected to supply the necessary funds to make the safeguards workable.

One is tempted to ask if all the blame for what happened to the Electra should be applied to Lockheed, to Allison, or to the CAA.

Quesada himself once was asked how much of the Electra's trouble could or should be laid on the doorstep of the federal government. His reply was interesting, to say the least, in view of his often expressed conviction that the federal government is there to protect the public:

"The problem of meeting the technical criteria of certification when an aircraft is built rests primarily with the Industry.

"The aircraft manufacturer is required to meet those criteria and produce a safe airplane. The FAA, well, it is physically impossible for the FAA to have within its own bosom the technical talents that exist within the industry. Problems such as have occurred in the Electra certainly can be laid to the manufacturer. He produced a bad airplane. I think the evidence is overwhelming in this respect.

"You could argue, and properly so, that the FAA should have detected this before tragedy struck. [He meant CAA; the FAA came into existence January 1, 1959. The CAA issued certificate number 4A22 to the L-188 on August 22, 1958.] However, we haven't reached that perfect world yet and the FAA is capable of making errors to the same extent as is the manufacturer. The basic error in this case, in my opinion, was made by the manufacturer. He designed the airplane within the criteria established. Admittedly, the FAA didn't detect it."

This is curious reasoning which leaves a question crying to be answered: Who was responsible for establishing what turned out to be inadequate criteria? The task of fixing blame for the Electra invariably goes around in a circle. It does not seem unfair to suggest that if there must be blame, it should be shared by many.

The Electra experience renewed an old demand by numerous air-safety experts. It was the proposal that all new airliners should be required to go through two years of cargo flights before they are allowed to carry passengers. The theory is that such a test period would uncover any major bugs.

The "make 'em fly cargo before they fly people" proposal was advanced in a *Reader's Digest* article. The author, a veteran airline captain, pointed out that the French Caravelle, a highly regarded medium-range jetliner, carried only cargo for two years. He said if the Lockheed Electra had undergone a similar break-in, the freak vibration weakness that caused two fatal crashes would have been exposed before any passengers were killed.

But U.S. air safety officials are largely opposed to the idea. They say it would cost exorbitantly and might not uncover any bugs.

Oscar Bakke, Director of Flight Standards for the Federal Aviation Agency before he became a regional administrator, puts it this way:

"It is impossible to establish any arbitrary time in which you can expose and eliminate design weaknesses. Two months or ten years of cargo flights might be as reasonable as two years."

What Bakke is arguing is that no one can predict when a major design bug is going to show up. There have been

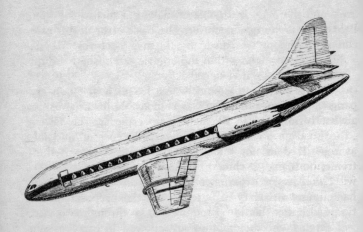

*Caravelle*

four such design boners in U.S. aviation history, with this
widely varying pattern of occurrence:

—The Lockheed Constellation which, after 16,500 hours
of flight time, came up with its electrical system weakness.

—The DC 6 which, after 31,000 hours of flight time,
came up with its flaw in the fuel transfer system,

—The Martin 202 which, after 19,214 hours, came up
with its structural weakness.

—And the Electra, whose vibration trouble didn't occur
until 78,996 hours of flight time were accumulated.

Suppose the first four Electras had been assigned to fly
cargo for two years. The maximum aircraft use is about ten
hours a day. In two years, those four planes would have
accumulated less than 30,000 hours of flight time—almost
50,000 hours under the time actually built up when the
Electra's bug developed.

Bakke points out that the Caravelle's two years of cargo
tests were financed by the French Government.

"Would the U.S. taxpayer be willing to foot such a bill?" Bakke asks. "Certainly the manufacturers or the airlines couldn't pay it."

Could they pay it?

Suppose the six-million-dollar Boeing 707 had had to fly cargo for two years before it was certificated to carry passengers. The airlines and Boeing would have had two alternatives:

—The airlines could have operated every 707 purchased as a cargo plane for the first two years, but only at a tremendous loss because a 100 percent cargo operation with such planes is highly unprofitable. Then they would have been faced with the necessity of expensive modifications when the planes were shifted to passenger service.

—Boeing and/or several airlines could have set aside four or five 707s for the test period. But what would have happened to the production line during that period? Could Boeing have continued building planes which the airlines couldn't use for two years? Or could Boeing have afforded to shut down production for two years?

Under either alternative, America's entry into the jet age would have been delayed two years while foreign airlines grabbed the major chunk of overseas business.

The cargo proposal is not new. It was first made in the mid-forties by the Air Line Pilots Association and has been renewed every time a new airliner is introduced.

The only effective answer is assurance that the FAA-industry test program is completely adequate.

FAA's certification requirements have been made even more rigid since the Electra's difficulties were solved. And it has the manpower that the CAA lacked. The agency is convinced that this still is preferable to the cargo-before-people proposal, which could cost millions without saving a single life.

There is one further argument against the proposal. Current government air safety rules apply equally to cargo and passenger flights. Pilots and planes are subject to the

same regulations whether they are carrying vegetables o
VIPs. The obvious reason for a single standard of safety i
that any plane crash could endanger lives and property or
the ground.

The cargo-before-people suggestion literally sets up a
double standard—and because of this it stands little chance
of acceptance.

For that matter the Caravelle, the only plane tha
went through a cargo-only period, still managed to de
velop minor bugs even after two years of such testing.
United, which is more than pleased with the twenty
Caravelles it has, reported these persistent mechanica
difficulties in the first four months of operation:

False engine-fire warnings, engine overheating, electrical power malfunctions, freezing and rupturing of water-
system lines, and troubles with the engine turbine blades.

The Caravelle, it might be noted, had gone through one
year of test flights, two years of cargo flights, and more
than a year of regular airline service in Europe before
United took delivery on its own fleet. This is not intended
as criticism of a magnificently designed airliner. It is merely
to repeat that bugs in an airplane, major and minor, can
hide perversely for surprisingly long periods. For example, what transport came up with a structural-fatigue
problem in 1962 after twenty-five years in airline service? None other than the DC-3, accepted as the most
perfectly engineered aircraft ever built, from a structural
standpoint!

The fatigue weakness was brought to light when a
National Guard DC-3 carrying Montana governor Nut-
ting lost a wing in moderate turbulence and crashed.
The structural area involved had been modified in commercial DC-3s as a precaution, but military models of
the plane were not affected by the civil modification
order.

The well-tested DC-8 and Boeing 707 jetliners also
suffered their share of unsuspected bugs that showed up

in spite of all the rigid tests. The former was plagued by hydraulic difficulties that did not develop until more than two years after the first DC-8 flew. The 707 prototype and its military version, the KC-135 tanker, compiled *four years* of operating experience before the plane entered commercial service. And still there were bugs in the hydraulic system.

The paradox of airplane design is that no test program, no matter how rigid and relentless, can quite duplicate the rigors of actual passenger service. Most bugs, it must be noted, are relatively minor and cause more embarrassment than danger. But it is seriously to be doubted if any specific period of cargo flights, whether two years or even ten years, is going to eliminate all of them. It is true that *some* difficulties might be spotted in a cargo-only operation, but the examples cited above show how impossible it would be to determine how long this operation should last.

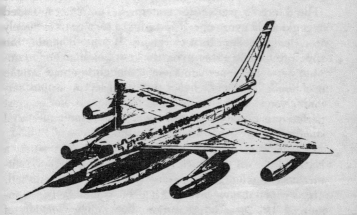

*B-58*

*   *   *

There is unanimous agreement that the Electra's problems have been solved. There may be other Electra accidents, but only because it is just an airplane, subject to human faults, mechanical failures, and perhaps mere fate. There probably will never be unanimous agreement on what caused Buffalo and Tell City. Whirl mode is the accepted theory of the majority and, barring the unexpected introduction of new evidence, will stand as the most likely "probable cause."

Other theories crop up from time to time. Captain Don Schulberg of Northwest, a stocky, youthful-looking Electra pilot, has put forth one which is intriguing, though unsubstantiated by the known facts.

Schulberg believes that both the Braniff and Northwest planes were destroyed by whirl mode—but that the triggering force, instead of a weakened outboard nacelle, was the sonic boom produced by a supersonic bomber or even fighter.

The Electra's propulsion system, he points out, is in effect a double gyroscope. The turbines turn counterclockwise, the propellers turn clockwise. If something should happen to tumble either gyro, the resulting uneven forces would be violent—perhaps violent enough to create whirl mode. It is Schulberg's belief that the Electra's opposite-rotating forces made it vulnerable to a sonic boom.

Schulberg is convinced there was a supersonic military plane, probably a B-58 bomber, in the vicinity of Buffalo and again near Tell City. Both communities are near Air Force bases. Not too much is known about the effects of sonic boom, although its shock wave has a demonstrated capability of breaking windows on the ground from thousands of feet up. The airstream shock wave emanating from a jetliner once took the wing off a small plane that got caught in its wake and, according to Schulberg's theory, the sonic boom could be even more destructive, depending on its proximity.

His chief evidence concerns the Buffalo crash. He recalls that six ground witnesses testified they first heard a
terrific explosion of such magnitude that they rushed outside. Then they looked up and saw a flash of light as the
Electra came apart. Schulberg holds that if the explosive
sound came from the Electra, they should have seen the
light first and *then* heard the sound, inasmuch as light
travels faster than sound. What he believes they actually
heard was a sonic boom *preceding* the Electra's breakup.

He further cites a "white light" seen by another ground
witness and theorizes that what the witness was watching
was a military jet afterburner in the process of ignition as
it started to move from subsonic to supersonic speed.
Schulberg's reconstruction is that the sonic boom hit the
number one propeller of the Braniff plane at a right angle,
bent it out of its normal rotation plane, and triggered
whirl mode. He thinks the same thing happened at Tell
City.

The CAB's reports on the two accidents stress the absence of any aircraft in the near vicinity of the airliners.
Schulberg notes, however, that there were two KC-135
tankers on a refueling mission the night of the Buffalo
crash, both assigned to the Carswell Air Force base, which
has a B-58 squadron and is only one hundred and twenty
miles from Buffalo. Another B-58 unit is based near Peru,
Indiana, one hundred and fifty miles from Tell City.

The big hole in his theory is the complete lack of
evidence that any supersonic military planes, B-58s or
otherwise, were flying anywhere near the ill-fated Electras.
Schulberg claims they could have been on secret missions
or test flights. Yet it is unlikely that the missions would
have remained secret during the course of the massive
Electra investigations. This would have involved an Air
Force conspiracy to avoid any responsibility for the two
accidents. And to go a debunking step further, there is no
evidence that a sonic boom could bend a steel propeller.

The interest of this one pilot in the story of the Electra,

however, is indicative of the never-ending controversy surrounding the plane. Every man connected with the two crashes has a million memories burned into his soul. There is one Northwest captain who was assigned to the Tell City investigation. He remembers the night he walked into a Tell City bar and was angered almost to the point of starting a fight. He thought everyone present was celebrating the accident—until another pilot reminded him that it was Saint Patrick's Day.

For Lockheed, the unhappy residue is financial as well as emotional. Not including the fifty-five million dollars in damage suits, Lockheed lost a conservative fifty-seven million dollars on the Electra project. Some of it may be regained, however. The Electra's assembly line is still in operation for production of the P3V, a Navy version of the prop-jet used as an anti-submarine patrol plane.

A total of one hundred and seventy-four Electras were built and sold. Contrary to many reports, Tell City did not

*P3V "Orion"*

sound the plane's death knell as a salable commercial transport. Lockheed had actually decided only a few hours before that crash occurred to cease Electra production when all current orders had been filled. The company was convinced the sales saturation point had been reached for a prop-jet of its size and performance. The public already was expressing a preference for pure jets.

Production ended with five Electras still unsold, but all five had been built for Capital, which canceled the order after it ran into an economic morass so deep that the airline could not have financed a Piper Cub. Eventually Braniff bought one, Pacific Southwest another, and the remaining three went to a new company organizing a sports-charter business. There was some cynical eyebrow-raising at the choice, but the company merely pointed out that one of the satisfied Electra operators happened to be the Los Angeles Dodgers, who had purchased an L-188 for team transportation.

Controversy has managed to cling to the Electra despite its cleansed reputation. In the spring of 1962, two FAA experts advanced the theory that the plane's engines make a sound like a mass of chirping crickets—thus attracting hungry starlings. They suggested that Allison modify the engines to eliminate the attraction. A substantial number of ornithologists promptly said the theory was for the birds.

Some tiny residue of prejudice also continues to cling. A National Football League team chartered an airliner for a transcontinental trip during the 1962 exhibition season. When several players heard the plane was an Electra, they protested to club officials. The airline had to substitute a DC-7.

# Postscript

As of mid-1990, there were ninety-five L-188s still flying throughout the world, the vast majority in cargo service. The last major U.S. airline to operate the Electra in regular passenger service was Eastern.

On November 1, 1977, EAL retired the last L-188 in its fleet from the Washington–New York Shuttle, even though the venerable prop-jet had proved to be the Shuttle's best all-around airplane. On more than one occasion, an Electra had beaten a DC-9 jet to its destination by as much as thirty minutes, an astounding feat inasmuch as the Electra was operating as an extra section that left *after* the DC-9. The Electra's ability to operate more efficiently at lower altitudes made the difference.

But the plane's maintenance costs had soared to the point where its versatility was no longer an important factor. It was costing Eastern $8000 to replace a propeller that had cost only $2700 when the aircraft was brand-new. Prop overhaul alone for the airline's last three Electras required a ten-man shop crew, and some replacement parts had to be built to order for an airliner that was averaging only two hours daily utilization.

In retrospect, the Electra story echoed the bitter truth of aviation's oldest axiom: In safety, nothing can be taken for granted. It was *not* a carelessly designed airplane, but its design did involve some wrong assumptions that cost

he lives of nearly one hundred people. If anything posi-
ive came out of this technological tragedy, it was that it
demonstrated what government-industry cooperation can
achieve in a crisis atmosphere. The solution of Buffalo and
Tell City and the subsequent corrective measures were
inspiring examples of such cooperation—in speed, scope,
and determination.

This is the true legacy of the plane called the Electra
and of the two disasters over Texas and Indiana. The
lessons taught have not always been learned well; design
flaws have plagued the DC-10's reputation and no manufacturer, engine or airframe, has been completely immune
from engineering mistakes. Yet overall, the design and
certification process for new airliners is at the highest
level of safety in aviation history, and the Electra experience played no small role in setting the stage for that
achievement.

Lockheed itself, sad to relate, has abandoned the commercial airliner field. Ironically, its final airline product
was its finest: the superb L-1011, victimized by a market
that could not viably accommodate both the L-1011 and
the DC-10.

Two years after the accident at Buffalo, Texas, the Richard Whites were still living on the farm where it all
started. The following March he suffered a heart attack
(his wife blamed it on the crash) and went into virtual
retirement. The vegetable patch where most of the Braniff
plane fell was turned into pasture land.

"Who would eat vegetables where people died?" Mrs.
White explained rather bitterly.

For years, another pasture a half-mile away was still
covered with tiny shreds of aluminum and other small
debris from Braniff Flight 542, Captain W. E. Stone commanding. But Stone's widow eventually remarried—an
American Airlines captain then flying Electras.

And in a way, that was the right ending for the Electra

story. In the close-knit fraternity of the air, they looked ahead to the promises and challenges of the future, rather than back on the mistakes and sorrows of the past.

Which is not just the story of the Electra.

It is the story of commercial aviation.

# A Note About the Author

Robert J. Serling is the former aviation editor of United Press International and the author of 19 published fiction and nonfiction works, including the best-selling *The President's Plane is Missing*. His first work, *The Probable Cause*, was a widely acclaimed study of air accidents and went through several printings as a Ballantine paperback.

Since its original publication in 1962, *The Electra Story* has become a classic aviation tale and one of the most eagerly sought books by collectors. It is significant that the two manufacturers involved in the Electra tragedy, Lockheed and Allison, both praised the book for its objectivity and fairness. And it came as no surprise that it was named the best aviation book of the year by the Aviation Space Writers Association which also awarded Serling the AWA's coveted James J. Strebig Memorial Award for "meritorious aviation reporting."

That honor is one of many Bob Serling has earned during his long writing career. He won the Strebig Award for an unprecedented second time in 1980, and in 1988 received the United Technologies' Lauren D. Lyman Award for Distinguished Aviation Writing—aerospace journalism's equivalent of a Pulitzer Prize. Special commendations from the Flight Safety Foundation, Sherman Fairchild Foundation, and Air Line Pilots Association are among his other honors.

Serling is a former member of the Flight Safety Foundation's Board of Governors and holds an honorary degree in Aeronautical Science from Embry-Riddle Aeronautical University. He resides with his wife and two children in Tucson, Arizona, where he is currently writing a history of Boeing.

# A Note About
# The Bantam Air & Space
# Series

This is the era of flight—the century which has seen man soar, not only into the skies of Earth but beyond the gravity of his home planet and out into the blank void of space. An incredible accomplishment achieved in an incredibly short time.

How did it happen?

The AIR & SPACE series is dedicated to the men and women who brought this fantastic accomplishment about, often at the cost of their lives—a library of books which will tell the grand story of man's indomitable determination to seek the new, to explore the farthest frontier.

The driving theme of the series is the skill of *piloting*, for without this, not even the first step would have been possible. Like the Wright Brothers and those who, for some 35 years, followed in their erratic flight path, the early flyers had to be designer, engineer, and inventor. Of necessity, they were the pilots of the crazy machines they dreamt up and strung together.

Even when the technology became slightly more sophisticated, and piloting became a separate skill, the quality of a flyer's ability remained rooted in a sound working knowledge of his machine. World War I, with its spurt of development in aircraft, made little change in the role of the flyer who remained, basically, pilot-navigator-engineer.

Various individuals, like Charles Lindbergh, risked their lives and made high drama of the new dimension they were carving in the air. But still, until 1939, flying was a romantic, devil-may-care wonder, confined to a relative handful of hardy individuals. Commercial flight on a large scale was a mere gleam in the eye of men like Howard Hughes.

It took a second major conflict, World War II, from 1939 to 1945, to provoke the imperative that required new concepts from the designers—and created the arena where hundreds of young men and women would learn the expertise demanded by high-speed, high-tech aircraft.

From the start of flight, death has taken its toll. Flying has always been a high-risk adventure. Never, since men first launched themselves into the air, has the new element given up its sacrifice of stolen lives, just as men have never given up the driving urge to go farther, higher, faster. Despite only a fifty-fifty chance of any mission succeeding, *still* the dream draws many more men and women to spaceflight than any program can accommodate. And still, in 1969, when Mike Collins, Buzz Aldrin, and Neil Armstrong first took man to the Moon, the skill of piloting, sheer flying ability, was what actually landed the "Eagle" on the Moon's surface. And still, despite technological sophistication undreamed of 30 or 40 years earlier, despite demands on any flyer for levels of performance and competence and the new understanding of computer science not necessary in early aircraft, it is piloting, *human* control of the aircraft—sometimes, indeed, inspired control—that remains the major factor in getting there and back safely. From this rugged breed of individualists came the bush pilots and the astronauts of today.

After America first landed men on the Moon, the Russian space program pushed ahead with plans for eventually creating a permanent space station where men could live. And in 1982 they sent up two men—Valentin Lebedev and Anatoly Berezovoy—to live on Solyut-7 for seven months. This extraordinary feat has been recorded in the diaries of pilot Lebedev, *Diary of a Cosmonaut: 211 Days in Space* by Valentin Lebedev.

The Bantam AIR & SPACE series will include several titles by or about flyers from all over the world—and about the planes they flew, including World War II, the postwar era of barnstorming and into the jet age, plus the personal histories of many of the world's greatest pilots. Man is still the most important element in flying.

Here is a preview of next month's volume in the
AIR & SPACE series:

# ZERO

by

## Martin Caidin

## 1

# The Sino-Japanese Incident

*At certain times in her history, economic, political, and* other implications have forced Japan into armed conflict with neighboring countries. Although such action may be justified, the nature of war demands from the belligerent nation a high cost in human lives, the drainage of natural resources, and the "judgment of God."

Universal intimacy with the horrors of war makes it superfluous to discuss in detail the misery of the vanquished; however, recent history illustrates clearly that the victor also may lose far more than he gains from war. For large countries in an economically sound condition, damage usually is confined to relatively small areas, and the economy suffers but little. For a nation such as Japan, however, the damaging effects of only one major defeat in war may be so far-reaching and so profound that a subsequent series of victories will be unable to offset the damage incurred in the previous defeat.

We feel that we can justify the thesis taught to the Japanese masses whereby they were, subsequent to the Sino-Japanese and Russo-Japanese wars, led to believe that Japan would not and could not lose a war. Be that as it may, the military and political leaders in whose hands lies the future of a nation should concentrate their efforts on devising means not merely of winning a war but of preventing defeat, should armed conflict prove inevitable. Should these national leaders be misled by the outward appearance of the armed might at their disposal and throw their nation into the cataclysm of war without an exhaustive study of the implications of their actions, they cannot themselves escape the consequences of their acts. Their actions are nothing short of outrageous or, in modern parlance, subversive, regardless of theoretical justifications.

It has been the tragedy of modern Japan that those great and humane statesmen who attempted to follow the principles of "fair play" in international conduct often met death, and that several cabinets composed of such men fell by the wayside before the pressure of the military cliques.

We, the Japanese, must never forget that it was criminal to permit this situation to exist; that because of this intolerable political blindness we pushed millions of our good neighbors into misery and suffering beyond the comprehension of most Japanese civilians; and, finally, that our own foolish actions hurled Japan into the present economic abyss from which she finds it so difficult to emerge. We must provide some form of compensation for those countries on which we have visited destruction; we must maintain the utmost vigilance to prevent the repetition of past mistakes.

Despite this attitude, so necessary to peaceful international conduct, there arise occasions when armed might is indispensable to a nation's welfare. Those persons who have been invested with their nation's military responsibility must, without regard to politics, do their utmost to execute the duties entrusted to them.

To meet its military requirements, a nation will strive for the most effective weapons and manpower. Several decades ago Japan recognized adequate airpower as the weapon most suited to solve its national defense problems and accordingly stressed the growth of that arm, notably in the naval field.

On July 7, 1937, the Sino-Japanese Incident flared on the Asian mainland, almost a quarter of a century after we had undertaken to develop our naval air power. At this time the Navy was prepared to counter any eventuality with this striking force:

## CARRIER STRIKING FORCE

### FIRST CARRIER DIVISION

Under command of Rear Admiral Shiro Takasu, in Ryujo:
Ryujo, Captain Katsuo Abe
    12 Type 95 carrier based fighters
    15 Type 94 carrier-based dive bombers
Hosho, Captain Ryunosuke Kusaka
    9 Type 95 carrier-based fighters
    6 Type 92 carrier-based attack bombers

### SECOND CARRIER DIVISION

Under command of Rear Admiral Rokuro Horie, in Kaga:
Kaga, Captain Ayao Inagaki
    12 Type 90 carrier-based fighters
    12 Type 94 carrier-based dive bombers

12 Type 89 carrier-based attack bombers
12 Type 96 carrier-based attack bombers

## LAND-BASED AIR FORCE

### FIRST COMBINED AIR FLOTILLA

Under command of Captain Mitchitaro Tozuka, at Taipei (later Shanghai):

*Kisarazu Air Corps*, Captain Ryuzo Takenaka
  6 Type 95 land-based attack bombers
24 Type 96 land-based attack bombers
*Kanoya Air Corps*, Captain Sizue Ishii
  9 Type 95 carrier-based fighters
18 Type 96 land-based attack bombers

### SECOND COMBINED AIR FLOTILLA

Under command of Rear Admiral Teizo Mitsunami, at Ohmura (later Shanghai):

*12th Air Corps*, Captain Osamu Imamura
12 Type 95 carrier-based fighters
12 Type 94 carrier-based dive bombers
12 Type 92 carrier-based attack bombers
*13th Air Corps*, Captain Sadatoshi Senda
12 Type 96 carrier-based fighters
12 Type 96 carrier-based dive bombers
12 Type 96 carrier-based attack bombers

| | | |
|---|---|---|
| *Total strength:* | 66 | carrier-based fighters |
| | 51 | carrier-based dive bombers |
| | 54 | carrier-based attack bombers |
| | 48 | land-based attack bombers |

219 combat-ready warplanes

There were also available the thirty scout and observation seaplanes of the coastal defense ship *Izumo*, the flagship of the Third Fleet (stationed at Shanghai); the seaplane tender *Kamoi;* and various cruisers.

When the fighting spread to Shanghai on August 13, 1937, our intelligence reported that the Japanese garrison in that city was completely encircled by a strong Chinese force, supported by three hundred planes based in the Nanking area. Additional reports revealed that a concerted Chinese attack could in a few days wipe out to the last man the Japanese marines who were isolated in Shanghai. The marine garrison faced overwhelming numbers of Chinese troops; since no airfield within Shanghai was usable, our men were denied local air coverage.

On August 14, following a series of sharp land battles, the Chinese planes opened bombing attacks against our forces in and around Shanghai. Even as the raids began, a single Type 90 scout-observation seaplane of the *Izumo* attacked the enemy formations, downing one fighter. This first aerial battle forecast greater commitments of planes by both sides.

On the evening of August 14, the Type 96 land-based attack bombers (Nells) of the Kanoya Air Corps based at Taipei (Formosa) attacked Chinese positions. On the following day Nells of the Kisarazu Air Corps from Ohmura Base on Kyushu Island began their bombing raids, and, commencing on the sixteenth, the carrier planes joined the rising tide of raids against the enemy's forces. These attacks of the Nells constituted the first "transoceanic" bombing raids.

For many years the Japanese Army and Navy had hidden their armament and weapons; the public saw only the obsolete models of heavy guns, warships, and planes. In contrast to this policy, other countries obviously attempted to frighten their enemies into submission through constant exhibition of their military forces. Knowledge of the true performance of foreign weapons was denied the public; the propaganda mills ground out exaggerated reports of the actual strength of each nation.

By importing many foreign aircraft and weapons, we in Japan were able to gauge approximately what these weapons could and could not do. By keeping our planes and other armament within our borders and free from prying eyes, we led the world to seriously underestimate the combat strength of our naval aviation.

The so-called transoceanic bombing missions of the Sino-Japanese Incident revealed for the first time the actual capabilities of Japanese warplanes. The long-distance raids by the Nell bombers, averaging two thousand kilometers (1250 miles) for each raid, exceeded by a considerable margin the previous maximum-range attacks of any country's planes. Further appreciation of this startling advance in aerial warfare was possible when it was revealed that these airplanes were carrying out their attacks in extremely poor weather, flying from Formosa and Kyushu against targets in and around Shanghai, Nanking, Hangchou, and other cities.

The elation which swept the Japanese populace with the announcements of the bombing was understandable. We had a powerful, long-range, fair-and-foul-weather, day-and-night bombing force. Our planes constantly set new records; the only air battles fought across an appreciable expanse of water up to this time had been those undertaken in World War I across the Straits of Dover and its vicinity.

Despite the obvious quality of our planes and the caliber of our pilots, the Navy's Air Force suffered heavy losses in the early days of the incident. There was much to be learned in the art of long-distance attack which could be acquired in peacetime, but the price the Chinese exacted for those lessons was severe.

We learned—almost at once, and with devastating thoroughness—that bombers are no match for enemy fighter planes. We lost many men as this lesson was administered, including Lieutenant Commander Nitta, Air Group Commander, Lieutenant (JG) Umebayashi and En-sign Yamanouchi of the land-based attack-bomber groups, and other pilots well known in Japan.

The planes of the aircraft carrier *Kaga* suffered disastrously. The twelve Type 89 carrier-based attack bombers, led by Group Commander Lieutenant Commander Iwai, left the *Kaga* on August 17 for a raid against Hangchou. Bad weather prevented a rendezvous with an expected fighter escort and near their target the bombers were attacked by a group of Chinese fighter planes. Eleven bombers, including the commander's, were shot down. Lieutenant (JG) Tanaka managed to bring his bullet-riddled and crippled bomber safely back to the carrier; otherwise, the fate of the attacking group would never have been known, and another bomber formation might have suffered a similar fate. Tanaka's report astonished the officers of the fleet, and immediate warnings were issued to all bomber groups to take special precautions against the defending Chinese fighters.

We discovered that when our fighter planes provided escort to, over, and from the target such incidents did not occur. Comparing the shattered unescorted bomber groups with the relatively unharmed formations which were protected by fighters, the Navy reacted quickly. The *Kaga* was ordered to return immediately to Sasebo and to receive a full complement of the new Type 96 carrier-based fighters (Claudes).

Although the fighters had never flown in service operations from an aircraft carrier, the gravity of the situation warranted the risk of accidents. In early September the Second Combined Air Flotilla, equipped with the powerful Claudes, returned to Shanghai.

In the Second Combined Air Flotilla were Lieutenant Commander Okamura, Lieutenant Commander Genda, and Lieutenant Nomura, three of Japan's outstanding veteran fighter pilots; later they were joined by another combat veteran, Lieutenant Nango. The flotilla's first raid against Nanking on September 18 was followed by wave after wave of attacks, made chiefly with dive bombers and the powerful Claude fighters.

The Chinese air force put up a desperate air defense, hurling fighters of international repute against the Mitsubishi fighter planes. Chinese pilots attacked the Claudes with such planes as the English Gloster Gladiator, the American Curtiss 75, and the Russian N-15 and N-16 fighters. There was no doubt about the outcome of the protracted aerial engagements; from the outset the Claudes proved their superiority in a series of air victories. Within two months of the initial attacks against the Chinese targets, the enemy's fighter planes disappeared from the arena; the last combat on December 2, when Lieutenant Nango's Claudes blasted ten N-16's from the sky over Nanking, was a glorious victory. All through October and November the Japanese people rejoiced at the brilliant combat successes of the Claudes, which battled numerically superior forces.

The Chinese moved their air-base facilities to rear areas beyond the flight range of the marauding Mitsubishi fighter planes, establishing new headquarters at Nanching in central China, about 335 miles southwest of Shanghai. Attacking their planes from Shanghai with Claude fighters required new tactics. Lieutenant Commander Genda, air staff officer of the 2nd Combined Air Flotilla, proposed that the Navy set up special refueling bases close to the Chinese lines to be used by the fighters on their way to the enemy.

Employing Type 95 land-based attack bombers as emergency transport planes, the Navy flew fuel and mechanics for the fighters into Kuangte Air Field. Although occupied by the Japanese Army, the airfield was partially isolated, since the enemy still controlled the supply lines. Our fighter planes landed at Kuangte for refueling, then resumed their flights for the Nanching area. Those planes with sufficient fuel to return directly to Shanghai flew nonstop from the target area; the remainder with short fuel reserves made another stop at Kuangte.

The novelty of the new tactics proved completely successful, as repeatedly our fighters made disastrous surprise raids against the unsuspecting Chinese. Japan gained a hero in this series of attacks; Flight Petty Officer Kashimura had just downed his second enemy plane in a single engagement when the falling fighter rammed the Claude, shearing off more than one third of its left wing. Through superb piloting Kashimura managed to return his crippled fighter to Shanghai.

The demands of battle forced the naval planes into unexpected situations for which they had not been trained. Carrier-based dive bombers, attack bombers, and Type 95 carrier-based fighters repeatedly reconnoitered, bombed, and machine-gunned enemy forces in direct cooperation with our army units, which were advancing steadily westward from the Shanghai area to Nanking. Although lacking in training and experience, the naval pilots performed these missions so successfully that they received the greatest praise of the ground units, who benefited materially from their supporting attacks.

These special operations were discontinued after three months of fighting, marked by the fall of Nanking. Many lessons were gained in the way of new tactics and operations from the campaign, especially (1) that air groups and combat planes trained at sea for sea duty can serve successfully without special training in any air campaign over land, and (2) that the key to success in any land or sea operation depends upon command of the air.

The outstanding combat successes of the Claude fighter planes ended a long-standing controversy in Japan, destroying once and for all the validity of the arguments of those who insisted upon retaining biplane-type fighters. Even with due consideration for its exceptional maneuverability, the short range and slow speed of the Type 95 carrier-based fighter doomed it to extinction. It required the final test of combat to determine which of these two fighter types would be the most effective in war.

The China air battles vindicated completely the Navy's insistence upon the strictest training for all pilots and air crews. Although the naval pilots were trained specifically for operations against enemy surface fleets, their quality enabled them to perform with an efficiency superior to that exhibited by our Army pilots. Conversely, it was also determined that pilots trained specifically for maneuvers over land experienced great difficulty in overwater operations, even in merely flying long distances over the ocean.

We discovered that the extended range of our Navy bombers opened new vistas of aerial warfare and that with these far-flying aircraft we could attack enemy positions far behind the front lines or while several hundred miles at sea. Most important of all, perhaps, we learned that certain types of air campaigns could not be strictly defined as either strictly "land" or "sea" battles, but required of the pilots the ability to fight under any conditions.

Despite these more obvious results of aerial warfare in China, the farsighted younger officers of the Navy Air Force encountered a solid wall of conservatism among the military hierarchy. The situation within the Army proved similar; there was little change in the basic concept of air power as an auxiliary to sea and land forces. Aware that they must first overcome the obstacles of outmoded thinking before they could hope to modernize our aerial weapons, our naval air officers again bent every effort to obtain greater authority and increased funds for their Air Force.

In the succeeding years, these efforts proved their worth: modern equipment, better training, and increased numbers of planes gave the Navy the strength of modern air power. Despite radical changes within its own organization, the Army failed to keep pace with the constant and rapid advances in air power achieved by the Navy, and was especially deficient in general reliability and ground maintenance. Except for a few plane types such as the Type 100 headquarters plane, far superior to any comparable Navy aircraft, the performance of the Army's planes fell below those of its sister service.

Despite vigorous attempts to modernize the Army's air training policies, it remained particularly deficient in overwater and night-flying capabilities. The Army Air Force never quite emerged from its position as the "crippled air force" whose dominion was confined entirely to the land.

Even as Japan drifted toward the Pacific War, men of foresight recognized the need for a land-based air power capable of operating under any conditions. These men, outside the military organization, failed in their efforts to convince the Army's leaders of their views.

We have often wondered about this misfortune of Japan, whose particular military, political, and social system did not permit the views of people outside the military hierarchy to affect the nation's armament. Certainly, we could have done much to improve the effectiveness of our air strength had we at least listened.

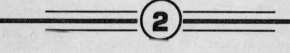

# Peace Attempts Fail— The Fighting Continues

*The war in China was now three years old. We discontinued* temporarily military operations in middle China, commencing with the occupation of Nanking in December of 1937. By the year's end the Japanese government was making every possible effort to settle politically the regrettable conflict between Japan and China. The attempts at negotiation failed completely, due primarily to the interruption of the Japanese Army hierarchy, as well as to the desire of influential Chinese parties to see the war continued. Indeed, in January, 1938, Army officers compelled Prime Minister Konoye against his will to announce: "We will not negotiate with the Nationalist Government of Chiang Kai-shek."

The inevitable happened; the war continued and no end appeared in sight. The Japanese people, concerned with the rapid spread of open fighting in China since July 7 of the previous year, still believed optimistically that despite the Prime Minister's obvious surrender to the Army, the war would soon end. Several leaders of our country publicly warned the government of the foreseeable grave consequences of extended fighting with China. A number of patriots in and outside of government service openly opposed the influential Army groups which, acting through the timorous prime minister, had so effectively diverted national policy and had committed the nation to war. These protests proved of little avail, as history relates.

Thus the fighting spread rapidly, soon enveloping most of China. In January of 1938 Japanese troops triumphantly concluded the Hankow Operation; thirteen months later they controlled Hainan Island and also temporarily and successfully halted the Shansi Campaign. In the interim our naval air units flew constant sorties, mainly in southern and central China. Once the Chinese air groups retreated beyond the range of the Type 96 carrier fighters to rebuild their shattered strength, the air war became a protracted struggle confined almost entirely to the bombing attacks of the Type 96 land-based attack bombers. Despite the best intentions of our commanders, the war situation demanded the presence of the naval air units at the Chinese front, a situation in which their maximum potentialities could not possibly be developed.

# 3

# Zero Fighters in China

*Following their advance in late 1938 to the Hankow Air* Base, the Navy Air Force flew close-support missions for Army troops and Navy surface forces with Type 97 carrier attack bombers (Kates) and with Type 99 carrier dive bombers (Vals). The Type 96 land-based attack bombers (Nells) bombed Chungking and other interior bases. The Type 96 carrier fighters (Claudes) defended our air bases and engaged enemy fighters whenever the Chinese pilots ventured within the range of the Claudes.

Between May and September of 1939, the Nells attacked Chungking from Hankow bases with twenty-two separate raids, aggregating an overtarget total of two hundred bombers. On November 4, 1939, Nells flew from the Hankow bases to attack Chengtu, and from late November to late December the Nells flew from Yucheng bases in Shansi to raid Lanchow (in Kansu).

The continuous aerial assaults noticeably weakened the Chinese Air Force's offensive power. Despite the effectiveness of the attacks, however, within six months we noticed definite signs of recovery. From mid-May to early September of 1940 Nells repeatedly battered the Chungking area. There were in the Hankow area in mid-1940 130 Type 96 bombers assigned to the four China-based air corps—Kanoya, Takao, the 13th, and the 15th. Every flyable airplane flew in each mission against Chungking for a total of 168 daytime attacks and 14 night raids, aggregating 3,717 bombers over target.

These were the heaviest raids of the China air war. On eight raids, Army Type 97s joined the Nells, aggregating seventy-two planes over target. The limited range of the Claude fighters prevented them from escorting the bombers to their objectives, where waiting Chinese fighters pounced upon the raiders. We suffered heavy losses: nine planes were destroyed or missing, and a total of 197 bombers were damaged. During some raids the percentage of lost or damaged bombers rose beyond the "prohibitive" figure of 10 percent. The Chinese fighters inflicted at least half the damage sustained by our bombers, while antiaircraft fire was responsible for the remainder. We could alleviate this unsatisfactory situation only by securing command of the air over the targets.

The Zeros were the answer. With their two machine guns and two 20-mm cannon they outgunned every airplane that opposed them. Their 300-mile-per-hour speed enabled them to pursue—and to catch—all enemy aircraft within their range. Combining the advantages of speed, rapid climb, excellent maneuverability, and heavy firepower, our pilots had in their new Zero fighter an airplane which shattered enemy opposition.

Besides the two skilled squadron commanders, Lieutenants Tamotsu Yokoyama and Saburo Shindo, and other well-known fighter pilots including Lieutenant (JG) Ayao Shirane, Flight Warrant Officers Koshiro Yamashita and Ichiro Higashiyama flew with the new planes.

On August 19, 1940, Lieutenant Yokoyama led a squadron of twelve Zero fighters on an escort mission of fifty Nell bombers over Chungking, but failed to encounter any Chinese fighters. The following day Lieutenant Shindo made another sweep over Chungking escorting fifty bombers, but again failed to find an opportunity to engage in combat. Our intelligence officers believed that the Chinese had already learned of the arrival of the Zeros in China and, accordingly, had carefully dispersed their planes. Despite the lack of action that our pilots coveted, the initial two combat flights proved valuable in that they enabled our pilots to become familiar with the combat area. The missions also established new world records for the combat flights of fighter planes: the Zeros flew a round trip of more than one thousand nautical miles.

By early September the Navy concluded its major offensive and expeditionary operations and recalled from the continent all units except the 12th Air Corps with Zero fighters, and the 13th Air Corps with several squadrons of Nell bombers stationed in the Hankow area.

On September 12, Lieutenant Yokoyama led twelve Zeros on an escort mission for twenty-seven Nells in an attack against Chungking. Unopposed in the air, the Zero pilots sighted five enemy planes on the ground at Shihmachow Air Field, and dove earthward in a strafing attack. The enemy planes were decoys, and the Zeros then strafed airfield structures and other military establishments. Despite the lack of active aerial opposition against the Zeros, photographs taken the same day by a Type 98 reconnaissance plane confirmed the presence of thirty-two Chinese planes on the bases about the city.

On September 13, thirteen Zeros under the command of Lieutenant Shindo and Lieutenant (JG) Shirane escorted Nell bombers from Hankow on the thirty-fifth raid of the 13th Air Corps against Chungking. After the bombing runs the pilots put into effect a long-planned ruse to lure the Chinese fighters out of hiding. The Nells turned and started for Hankow, accompanied by the fighter planes. Approximately at two o'clock in the afternoon, with our bombing-force already out of sight of the city, our reconnaissance plane radioed Lieutenant Shindo that Chinese fighters had appeared over Chungking.

The Zeros wheeled, climbing for altitude as they returned to the city and the unsuspecting Chinese fighters. Diving out of the sun, the Zeros swarmed over the Chinese pilots, spreading havoc with their machine guns and cannon. Within thirty minutes our pilots cleared the sky of all the Chinese fighters, later identified as twenty-seven Russian-made N-15 and N-16 airplanes.

Japan gained a new hero in Flight Warrant Officer Koshiro Yamashita, who in this single combat became an ace by destroying five enemy fighters. Flight Petty Officer (2nd Class) Oki, despite damage to his fuel tanks, pursued and destroyed an N-15 fighter. Two desperately evading enemy planes smashed into and exploded against a mountainside. Utterly confused by the flashing, swirling Zeros, three Chinese pilots hastily bailed out of their undamaged fighters. With the last enemy plane cleared from the sky, Warrant Officer Yamashita and Petty Officers Kitahata and Yoneda flew to Paishihyi Air Field, strafing and burning several Chinese planes which were just returning from other missions. Our pilots were overjoyed. Only four Zeros suffered light damage, and every one of our pilots escaped injury.

Vice-Admiral Shigetaro Shimada, the Commander-in-Chief of the China Area Fleet, immediately dispatched a special commendation to the Zero Fighter Squadron, which stated:

*SPECIAL COMMENDATION*

TO: THE 12TH AIR CORPS FIGHTER SQUADRON COMMANDED BY LIEUTENANT SABURO SHINDO:

ON 13 SEPTEMBER 1940 THIS SQUADRON MADE A SUCCESSFUL LONG-RANGE FLIGHT OVER THE MOUNTAINOUS SUCHUAN-SHENG (SZECHWAN PROVINCE) AREA, ESCORTING THE CHUNGKING BOMBING EXPEDITION OF THE LAND-BASED ATTACK BOMBER GROUP. AFTER COMPLETING THEIR ESCORT MISSION AND APPEARING TO LEAVE THE TARGET AREA FOR THE PURPOSE OF LURING ENEMY FIGHTERS FROM HIDING, THE SQUADRON

RETURNED TO CHUNGKING TO ATTACK A NU-
MERICALLY SUPERIOR ENEMY FIGHTER FORCE,
SUCCEEDING IN DESTROYING ALL ENEMY FIGHTER
PLANES THROUGH GALLANT AND COURAGEOUS
COMBAT. THIS OUTSTANDING SUCCESS DESERVES
THE *DISTINGUISHED MILITARY MERIT*.

I HEREBY AWARD THIS DIPLOMA OF MERIT.
OCTOBER 30, 1940.

> SHIGETARO SHIMADA
> COMMANDER-IN-CHIEF
> CHINA AREA FLEET

Obviously the inability of the Chinese pilots to present
a determined front to the attacking Zero fighters, accentu-
ated by two crashing enemy planes and the three pilots
who needlessly bailed out, contributed heavily to the one-
sided victory of September 13. Much of the credit, however, rested directly with the Zero fighter which, by virtue
of its superior flight range, staying power, high speed,
heavy firepower, and unexcelled maneuverability, imparted
to our pilots a tremendous advantage in dogfighting. This
was enhanced, of course, by the superior flying ability of
our pilots.

Informed of the brilliant first combat success of the Zero
fighters, Vice-Admiral Teijiro Toyota, Chief of the Naval
Bureau of Aeronautics, forwarded a letter of appreciation
(reproduced below) to each of the three companies—
Mitsubishi, Nakajima, and Dai Nihon Heiki (the Japan
Weapons Company)—which had manufactured the airframes,
engines, and 20-mm cannon. The Navy expressed its
great satisfaction with its new fighter by granting the
Nakajima company a large production order for Zero fighter
airframes.

## LETTER OF APPRECIATION

TO: MR. KOSHIRO SHIBA, CHAIRMAN
   BOARD OF DIRECTORS
   MITSUBISHI HEAVY INDUSTRY COMPANY, LTD.


THE RECENT OUTSTANDING SUCCESS OF THE 12TH AIR CORPS ZERO FIGHTER SQUADRON IN ATTACKING AND DESTROYING TWENTY-SEVEN CHINESE FIGHTERS OVER CHUNGKING ON SEPTEMBER 13, 1940, WITHOUT LOSS TO OUR AIRPLANES, IS DUE IN GREAT PART TO THE EXCELLENT PERFORMANCE OF THE ZERO FIGHTER AIRPLANE.

I HEREBY EXPRESS MY SINCERE GRATITUDE, AND THE GRATITUDE OF THE NAVY, FOR THE OUTSTANDING AND MERITORIOUS WORK OF YOUR COMPANY IN COMPLETING WITHIN A SHORT DEVELOPMENT TIME THIS EXCELLENT FIGHTER.

   SEPTEMBER 14, 1940
      TEIJIRO TOYOTA
      *VICE-ADMIRAL*
      *CHIEF, NAVY BUREAU OF AERONAUTICS*


Encouraged by the success of the Zero fighters against the enemy planes over Chungking, later in the afternoon of September 13, the 12th Air Corps launched the first attack against the city with Val bombers, flying from Ichang Air Base. Two days later, Kate bombers also flew from Ichang to attack Chungking. With its newly won command of the air over the Chinese objectives the Zeros made it possible for the Navy to apply all of its available bomber force against the enemy. On September 16, six Zero fighters attacked and destroyed a single large Chinese plane over Chungking; this was their last combat engagement for the month. Our pilots and mechanics devoted the final two weeks of the month solely to maintenance, preparing for the forthcoming flights deep within enemy territory to where the Chinese planes had fled.

On October 4, Lieutenants Yokoyama and Shirane led eight Zeros on an escort mission for twenty-seven Nells of the 13th Air Corps in their first raid against Chengtu in Szechwan Province. The two formations broke through thick clouds over the city at 2:30 P.M., and the bombers inflicted heavy damage on their targets. Unopposed in the air, the Zeros attacked nearby Taipingsu Air Field, shooting down five N-16 fighter planes and one SB bomber. Our pilots then strafed airplanes and airfield installations.

With ground facilities burning and Chinese personnel scattered from the field, Flight Warrant Officer Higashiyama and Flight Petty Officers Hagiri, Nakase, and Oishi landed on the field while the remaining Zeros flew top cover. Leaving their planes with engines running, the four pilots attempted to set afire the remaining undamaged Chinese airplanes. The fierce gunfire of returning Chinese troops forced them to abandon their plan and to take off immediately.

The Zeros again had struck hard, shooting down five fighters and one bomber, burning nineteen additional planes on the ground, and damaging four others, for a total confirmed kill of twenty-five enemy planes destroyed. Only two Zeros received light damage. Again Admiral Shimada forwarded a special commendation to the Corps.

The following day, October 5, Lieutenant Fusata Iida led seven Zeros in strafing attacks against Fenghuangshan Air Field near Chengtu. Our pilots set afire six large and four small planes and damaged two additional large aircraft. Fourteen decoys were burned.

As a consequence of these attacks, the backbone of Chinese air strength in the Chungking and Chengtu areas was broken. For weeks afterward the skies over these two cities were conspicuously free of enemy planes.

Immediately prior to the initial combat successes scored by the Zero fighters, elements of our Army and Navy were enabled to advance into French Indochina as a result of diplomatic negotiations with the French Vichy Government. (Although our entry into French Indochina resulted from diplomatic-political negotiations with France, this action eventually created strong friction between Japan and the United States, Great Britain, and other nations in the Allied fold. It could accurately be described as the first noticeable move in a series of events which finally resulted in the Pacific War.)

Our naval air units stationed in southern China flew immediately to their new bases in northern French Indochina. The proximity of these new stations to Chinese targets enabled us to launch single-engine bombers to attack Kunming, an area of great strategic importance in southwestern China which previously could be reached only by the long-range Nells. As soon as the French air bases could receive them, squadrons of the 14th Air Corps' Claude fighters, Kate attack bombers, and Val dive bombers were transferred to their new facilities. The 12th Air Corps in Hankow detached one squadron of Zero fighters, transferring them to French Indochina for long-range escort work.

On October 7, seven Zero and nine Claude fighters escorted a group of Val dive bombers to Kunming. Nearly twenty enemy fighter planes opposed the Zeros and Claudes, which definitely destroyed thirteen enemy planes and probably destroyed another. The Vals wrecked four enemy planes on the ground.

On December 12, seven Zero fighters escorted ten dive bombers and two bomb-carrying reconnaissance planes in an attack against Siangyun. Our fighters strafed and destroyed twenty-two enemy planes on the ground. From October 8 to the end of December, Zeros flew an additional twenty-two sorties, in which they definitely shot down two enemy planes.

While the Indochina-based planes attacked southern Chinese targets, on October 10, the Double Ten Festival Day of China, the 12th Air Corps Zeros in the Hankow area raided Chungking without encountering enemy opposition. On October 26, eight Zeros caught a large group of Chinese planes over Chengtu, destroying five enemy fighters, one transport plane, and four other types. On December 30, eight Zeros returned to Chengtu for their fourth attack, sweeping in a strafing attack over the Fenghuangshan, Taipingssu, Shuanglin, and Wenchiang airfields. They burned eighteen enemy planes, and wrecked fifteen others by cannon fire. The Zeros also set afire one large fuel storehouse and shot up other ground installations. Only two of our fighters suffered damage from antiaircraft fire.

Thus ended the year 1940 and the Zero fighter's baptism in combat. It drew first blood in an almost miraculous fashion, for in the period from August 19 to the end of the year the Zeros ran up this record:

Number of attacks made ........................ 22
Total number of planes used ..................... 153
Chinese planes shot down (one probable) .......... 59
Chinese planes destroyed (air and ground) ........ 101
Number of Zeros damaged by enemy fire ........ 13
Number of Zeros lost ........................... 0

However brilliant these combat successes, and however outstanding the record of our Navy Air Force in China, from the first transoceanic bombing of 1937 to the close of 1940, our pride can be justified only from the military standpoint.

No Japanese citizen can recall the events of these years and find justification for the *national* conduct of our country. No one can deny the record, for history will relate only that Japan forced her friendly neighboring nations into an unreasonable and unnecessary war, transformed their fields and cities into battlegrounds, and visited misery and deprivation on millions of innocent people.